Stop Smoking
with
Release for Life

By Graham Foster

Published by: Release for Life, 64 Southampton Road,
Portsmouth, PO6 4RX, UK.

Release for Life

Copyright © 2010 by Graham Foster

First edition published in paperback form 2003
ISBN 978-095448400-2.

Second edition re-published in paperback form as "Stop Smoking with Release for Life" in 2010
ISBN 978-0-9544840-1-9

Published by Release for Life.

Please note that much of this publication is based on personal experience and anecdotal evidence. Although the author and publisher have made every reasonable attempt to achieve complete accuracy of the content in this Guide, they assume no responsibility for errors or omissions. Also, you should use this information as you see fit, and at your own risk. Your particular situation may not be exactly suited to the examples illustrated here; in fact, it's likely that they won't be the same, and you should adjust your use of the information and recommendations accordingly.

Special thanks to Jamie for telling me to do it. Louise Hoare for extensive editing and contributions. Gill Humphreys for proofreading. And my good friends Martin and Siamak for their support, love and encouragement.

CONTENTS

Part 1

Preparation

How to use this course

The sole aim of this course is to help you break free from your addiction to nicotine. It has been conceived and written with this one aim in mind. The writer is a nicotine addict like you who has broken free from the addiction. Please consider the writing in this book to be like a personal conversation with you on a familiar level about a shared experience – addiction to nicotine. This is not a course about just how to stop smoking. Anyone can stop smoking, just get yourself locked up for a few days and you will have stopped. The trouble is you are more than likely to start again because stopping smoking is not the answer to nicotine addiction. If it was there would be no problem and no need for a course such as this, in fact you would not be smoking now if the answer was simply to stop smoking. The answer to nicotine addiction is to tackle the addiction so that you no longer smoke because you no longer wish or need to smoke and you feel this way permanently, for the rest of your life. This course will provide you with that answer.

Before we go any further I just want to explore with you what freedom really means. It means liberation, release – for life. Once you are released from your slavery your life changes. Smoking ties you down in many small ways and in some big ways. It ties you down emotionally. The endless circle of withdrawal and relief is an emotional pattern. It's familiar and comforting and it is something smokers do more when confronted with difficult or painful natural human emotions. It is an avoidance that leads to an emotional half life, or at least an emotional 'less than' life. How can you truly experience a feeling when you are in your

9

comforting withdrawal/relief circle? Smokers smoke much more when they are experiencing grief or loss or anxiety. Smoking also ties you down psychologically. Most smokers at some stage, and this can be quite early on for some, become bitter and resentful that they are stuck in this addiction. This is bound to have an effect on all or some areas of life. Smokers can feel stuck in their lives. This is often just a feeling, no matter what is going on in their lives they can still feel stuck. Smoking sets you up with a mind-frame of stuck-ness. You can be a successful film star with a glittering career, but you can still feel stuck and frustrated. I'm not saying smoking is the cause of this kind of mind-frame but it is easy to see that the constant smoking reflects and very strongly supports such a mind-frame. People who have truly become free from their addictions often experience freedom in all sorts of other ways. Freedom to go anywhere, freedom to experience, freedom to break free from other damaging situations in their lives, freedom to change, freedom to grow, freedom to love and freedom to be themselves without having to hide behind or within an addiction.

Addiction is slavery and its companions are resentment, frustration, ill-health, poverty, death, self loathing, low self-esteem, lethargy and fear. Liberation is freedom and its companions are hope, release, health, energy, greater wealth, living life to the full, self love, high self esteem, energy, strength and courage.

The addiction to nicotine is a complex matter. If the answer was simple then this course would be much smaller. The complexity of nicotine addiction has been broken down so that each and every element is covered in a simple to understand way. The course is long, because it seeks to cover all of the elements of the addiction and it does this in a way that is easy to understand. When you understand all the elements of how nicotine addiction works, it can no longer work on you, you can no longer be addicted. You can be released for life.

It is better to read the course while you are still smoking because you will find it easier to take in the information you need to become free if you are not fretting because you have stopped smoking. To illustrate this point I will tell you a little story. I once asked a friend of mine how he stopped smoking. He told me that he woke up one day and he couldn't find one single reason to smoke a cigarette and he has never smoked since. He suffered no withdrawals whatsoever. How annoying! The point to this story is that for whatever reason he awoke with no addiction illusions to keep him smoking. No reasons to smoke. This course is intended to destroy all your addiction illusions to leave you with no reasons to smoke just like my friend. This has more chance of success if your attention is not diverted by you trying to stop while you are reading the course.

Near to the end of the course you will be asked to smoke your last cigarette. This is an important element of the letting go process but what is important for you to understand right now is the timing of that last cigarette. To read and understand this course may take you a few hours or a few days or even a few weeks depending on how much time you have and how important this issue is for you. The best way to help yourself is to try to read this course as quickly as you can. I don't mean try to speed up your reading, or to not go over bits that you had a little difficulty understanding. What I mean is that it is better to devote a lot of time to it in as big a block as you can. It is better to read the course over a shorter time span as possible rather than read a little every other day for weeks. This is not bedtime reading. If you can devote two or three days to it so that your last cigarette is at the end of a block of time spent reading it, so much the better. If this is not easy to do for you then that's ok but be prepared to have difficulty in your smoking while you are reading the course. This is ok too. Being free from the addiction means being free and ultimately, however you work through this course you can be free.

The course is in four parts.

Part 1 - Preparation

Introduction – The part you are reading now.

Identification – Where I identify common ground with you.

Opening your mind – The key to understanding the information.

Part 2 - Barriers

What is addiction.

Issues – relax; concentrate; taste nice; after meals etc.

Part 3 - Illusions

Working through – Learning a process of freedom.

Other issues, problems and challenges.

Part 4 - Release

Last Cigarette

The first part is very short, it is to prepare you for what is to come. The second part shows you the process of nicotine addiction and how this process is at the root of so many addiction illusions. The third part is the largest part and it shows you a way of working through the addiction so that you can be permanently free with no suffering and it goes through more addiction illusions and challenges that arise immediately after you have stopped smoking. The fourth part is the very last part of the journey to your world of freedom, the last cigarette.

Apart from just reading words and looking at pictures there are some written and verbal exercises for you to do as well. You will need a pen and some paper or a notepad. This course is interactive. You will be asked to interact with the course by doing exercises and affirmations. These exercises and affirmations are designed to help you develop new thoughts and new patterns of thinking. This requires your active participation by doing the exercises and affirmations as fully as you can. As well as developing new thoughts, the exercises will also reinforce your understanding and retention of the information by helping your mind see it from different angles and perspectives and in different ways. If you have a practical problem about reading things out loud then say them in your mind with your eyes shut instead. Take as much time as you can and make as much effort as you can in doing all the exercises. The more work you do, the better for you.

Welcome

The very first thing I wish to say to you is that you are a brave and courageous person. I know this because it takes courage to begin a process of freedom from any addiction. I respect and applaud you for the love and commitment you are currently showing for yourself.

If you have tried stopping smoking before you may have a sense of shame for failing or you may have a greater fear of failing again. Let me assure you that every failed attempt is a useful tool and it doesn't matter how many times you have failed to stop in the past. I will be referring to those failed attempts during the course of this course so that you can identify with certain thoughts and feelings. In this way those failed attempts become a current, useful tool. Also, if you have failed before then clearly your motivation and courage is very great if you are still trying and I respect you for that.

This course is designed to help you become free from nicotine addiction. Sometimes, soon after you have smoked your last cigarette you may experience some feelings of panic or fear. Though you find this very difficult to believe right now, the truth is, it is very unlikely after working through this course that you will experience any fear or panic. But let's just say that you may have some fear that you might experience some sudden feelings of fear or panic. We are going to learn an effective tool to deal with this fear - a conscious thought will always over-ride a feeling and one such conscious thought will certainly help you get through any such feelings you are currently afraid of. The conscious thought I want you to learn is this:-

These feelings and this confusion will pass whether I smoke or not.

You may already know this truth. What we are going to do during the course of this book is to build and strengthen this thought so that it becomes an automatic reaction. We do this while we are still smoking so that there are no panic feelings associated with the new belief. We are going to reinforce this belief in our minds by the use of repetition. Throughout the course I will be asking you to repeat this belief six times, one after another. It is the most uncomfortable thing I will be asking you to do. Everything else is easy in comparison so please find the courage to do this no matter how silly you may feel at first. I want you to say this phrase out loud, as loud as you can six times in a row. I want you say it without any doubt about it and with absolute certainty and conviction. One of the things you can also try is to put more emphasis on different words such as:-

These feelings and this confusion will pass whether I smoke or not.
These feelings and this confusion will pass whether I smoke or not.
These feelings and this confusion will pass whether I smoke or not.
These feelings and this confusion will pass whether I smoke or not.
These feelings and this confusion will pass whether I smoke or not.
These feelings and this confusion will pass whether I smoke or not.

Another thing you can do is to write it down six times as if you were doing lines at school. Please trust me on this and do it whenever it comes up.

There are various methods to help people become free from the addiction to smoking. This course uses a tried and tested approach to addiction. The basic premise is that we smoke for a set of reasons. We have reasons to smoke so we smoke. One of the main problems with all addictions is the denial. Drug addicts deny they are drug addicts and so do nicotine addicts. The next major obstacle is developing a desire to give up. Once this obstacle is overcome and a strong desire to give up is achieved, many addicts find they cannot give up and they do not know why. The fundamental mistake people then make is to focus on the reasons why they should NOT be smoking, all the negatives. The truth is that people do not smoke because of all the reasons they shouldn't smoke, people smoke because of the reasons they have FOR smoking. Addicts who cannot give up are often confused and bemused as to why they find it so difficult or impossible and even when they do give up for a time, they start again. They are confused because they focus on why they should not smoke rather than looking at the issues of why they do smoke. For example,

I am stopping smoking because it is bad for my health.
I am stopping smoking because it is costing me too much money.
I am stopping smoking to prove to you and to myself that I can.
I am stopping smoking because I feel stupid for carrying on doing it.
I am stopping smoking because most of my friends don't smoke anymore.
I am stopping smoking because it is setting a bad example for my kids.
I am stopping smoking because my work colleagues see it as being unprofessional.

I am stopping smoking because I feel embarrassed about doing it these days.
I am stopping smoking because my doctor says I could lose my leg if I don't stop.
I am stopping smoking because . . . and so it goes on.

I have some bad news for you in case you didn't already know. All the reasons in the world why you shouldn't smoke will not stop you smoking. I'll repeat that again because sometimes when somebody says something that goes against what I have always believed, my mind can decide not to really hear it properly. **All the reasons in the world why you shouldn't smoke will not stop you smoking.**

The key to permanent freedom from this addiction is to look at all the reasons smokers smoke and work through those reasons so that they are no longer reasons. If you end up not having a reason to smoke, then you will not smoke. You will not smoke because you no longer have a reason to smoke. You may think you don't have a reason to smoke right now but as you go through the course you might find that some of the reasons you do smoke will come up and you will realise that you did have reasons to smoke after all and you just needed a little new information to see that.

You will find I talk about myself a lot and you might gain the impression that I am totally self obsessed. Well there are a number of reasons why I will be talking about myself a lot. Firstly, much of this course will be dealing with illusions versus truth, i.e. lies versus truth. The only genuine truth I know is that which my own experience is. For me to suggest that my truths are exactly the same as your truths would be less than honest and I might seem judgemental or presumptuous. Certainly many of our truths and misconceptions relating to smoking will be the same but because we are all individuals there are always differences. So I will be sharing with you my truths in the hope that you may identify with them. It is your identification of our shared truths that will set you free. If you want to get the most out of this experience look for the similarities between you and I, not the differences. If you focus on the differences you will simply be resisting the process of becoming free. To give yourself the very best chance, try and find all the similarities. For example, if I share with you that I chain smoked for years, it may be that you have not chain smoked for years. Simply leaving it at that will not help you. What is best for you to do is to identify those particular times you have chain smoked.

So, I share about myself because that is the only truth I have. The other reason, of course, is because I am totally self obsessed.

Essentially this course is about going on a journey through your mind, through all the illusions you have about smoking, so that you can be aware of all those issues and illusions and therefore be free from them. You will be presented with all the common illusions to do with this particular addiction throughout the course of the book. So what do I mean by being aware and therefore free? There is a path ahead of you of living smoke free. It is littered with holes, booby traps and trip wires. You will not trip or fall because you are aware they are there and you will see them all. You will become so aware that not even you will be able to con yourself any more. And you will be free. Make no mistake, if you have no illusions about smoking and you have no belief that you need to or have any pleasure in smoking, then you will feel no compulsion to smoke at all. You

18

will have faced all your thoughts and beliefs and feelings about smoking so that they cannot come back to haunt you.

Throughout this course I will be repeating myself time and time again. This is because I am planting new thoughts in your mind and one way to do this is repetition. Repetition helps you remember. Another process I will be using is getting to the same conclusions from different starting points. You will hear me guide you to the same answer to different questions. This is because the fundamental core issues that keep smokers trapped in the addiction are far less numerous than all the illusions surrounding them. So the same fundamental core answers apply to a whole range of different issues. As each thought you currently have leads to a smoke, each thought after this course will lead to the truth and to freedom from addiction.

Who am I?

What qualifications do I have and why do I think that this will work?

My name is Graham Foster. What qualifications do I have? I've got a few O levels and a couple of A levels and a degree in music and I even have a counselling skills course from my local technical college under my belt. But those aren't the qualifications that pertain to what we're doing today. So what qualifications do I have with regard to addiction? Well, I'm an alcoholic, a drug addict and I used to smoke like a chimney. I had my last drink and my last narcotic substance in March 1995 and I smoked my last cigarette in October 2000. My life journey has been devastated by addiction and in order to recover from this I have had to become an expert on the subject.

In view of my long-term career and recovery expertise in drug and alcohol addiction, wouldn't it be better if I concentrated my efforts in helping heroin addicts or alcoholics? Start up a treatment centre or something? Well I have, I am the Director of Addiction Recovery Centre in Portsmouth, UK, but let me first offer you a new perspective on these issues. A few hundred people a year die from using heroin. But let's break that down a little further. Of the very few people who die from heroin, a good proportion of these are suicides, there is actually a choice: they are intentional overdoses. Of the rest, it is usually unintentional overdose due to the drug being unreliable in strength or quality because the drug is illegal. Even then, the total number of deaths from heroin use is only a very small proportion of the total number of people who use heroin regularly. Heroin itself is not a killer drug. It ruins lives because of all sorts of chemical and social reasons, but the fact is, it is not the killer drug the media would have us believe. It is estimated that nicotine, on the other hand, directly kills 25%, a quarter of people who smoke it. Or to put it another way, the same amount of people who die from heroin each year die from nicotine each day. Today there will be hundreds of nicotine related deaths. That is the major reason why I choose to focus much of my time and energy on helping people to break free from nicotine as well as other substances. Another reason is that even though I have suffered from addiction to other substances, in my personal experience I found the nicotine addiction the hardest from which to break free. That's why I did it last.

My smoking career

When I was fifteen years old I was one of those people who were not going to take up smoking. My best friend and I were not going to smoke even though many of our friends were smoking. We went on a school trip to Germany where, because of being able to get alcohol at a younger age, we got drunk quite a lot. It was in one of these drunken states that we came upon the idea of trying a cigarette. We didn't think just trying it would make us hooked but we wanted to know what was so good about it that made people want to do it so many times a day for most of their lives. It was also partly the risk of the naughtiness that excited us. And there was also the issue of us being able to say to our friends we tried it, we can inhale without coughing and spluttering, even though we would choose not to become full time smokers.

The first one or two we didn't inhale but as we became more drunk we began inhaling just a bit. When we started inhaling properly we felt nauseated and dizzy and tried to resist coughing but of course we coughed anyway. All the symptoms of rejection our bodies were giving us, such as coughing and dizziness, we translated as a pleasurable 'high' which was probably an acquired taste. After all, there must be a better sensation than this but you must have to smoke quite a few before you learn to enjoy it and get out of it whatever it is people get out of it.

So we tried again the next night and the next night and the next. We felt proud of ourselves for being able to smoke and yet we weren't hooked so the fear of becoming hooked had gone. This is one of the reasons why smoking hooks so many people. It is actually not so addictive in itself. You cannot be addicted to just the chemical like you can with heroin. The addictive aspect of nicotine is so weak it takes time for any addiction to appear and even when it does it is mainly the illusions that form the addiction, not the chemical. Then it was time to go home. We both agreed that when we got home we would not smoke again except just the once to prove to Phil and Martin and that lot that we could smoke, but we choose not to. The memory is a little hazy after that but it wasn't long before I remember being quite astonished and very worried that every time I decided not to smoke any more, after a while I would experience a panic attack and smoke again.

I was never a happy smoker. I would try to stop time and time again, yet I just continued to smoke more and more. Most of the time I just accepted it but I always felt that one day I would stop. I tried cold turkey, I tried going on holiday, and I tried staying in the bedroom. I tried nicotine gum and patches and inhalers, I even tried acupuncture and hypnotism. For the last few years of smoking I smoked roll-ups because I just could not afford real cigarettes. During various attempts to stop smoking I would often find myself emptying the bins on the kitchen floor trying to find dog ends from previously emptied ashtrays because I just needed a little bit of a smoke to get me through. It never worked. Eventually I was helped to freedom. Through looking at all the illusions and reasons why about the addiction, I was released for life.

I smoked because I wanted to identify myself with people who smoked. They seemed to be more adventurous and less sensible. They tended to have the same interests as me. I also smoked because I enjoyed it so much. The feeling I got when I lit up, especially if I hadn't had one for a while, was wonderful. Smoking was one of the few pleasures I had in life; it gave me relief from life's difficulties. The thought of not smoking was a fearful thought for me. I had heard that your sense of smell improves and I really didn't want to be able to smell a lot of things any better, particularly bodily or toilet-y smells, mine or other peoples. Whenever I did try to stop smoking I went nuts and ended up smoking again anyway. Stopping smoking became very fearful and each time I doubted whether to light up a cigarette the memory of going nuts made that cigarette more needed and somehow more of a comfort and pleasure. I couldn't imagine what you do with your hands if you don't smoke. Smoking helped me relax. I couldn't imagine being relaxed without smoking. Also, if I had any work to do that required concentration, I couldn't imagine being able to concentrate without smoking; smoking helped me concentrate. I needed to smoke to face situations that were important to me or anxiety producing like interviews or medical appointments. I couldn't imagine dealing with them without smoking. Smoking helped me get through.

Part 2

Barriers

Release for life

This course is certainly not about trying to get to a stage where you can live your life without smoking by struggling through and staying not smoking one day at a time. The sole aim of this course is to help you to be free. To have complete and permanent freedom from all the head mess that comes with smoking and trying to give up that you have been living with for years. To sort it out and get it wholly settled once and for all so that it never again is an issue in your life. Complete, total and permanent freedom from the whole thing.

As you go through the course it will bring up all kinds of thoughts and feelings that perhaps you were not aware had such importance to you. When something you have heard creates in you a reaction on a feelings level, use a pen and pad and jot it down. Having a feelings reaction is a good indication that this particular issue is important to your sub-conscious. Some of these feeling reactions will feel like shame. Shame being what it is you will instinctively not want to look at it, bring it up, or write it down because that is the nature of shame. Please trust that no matter how ashamed you feel this is simply a reflection of what is important to your sub-conscious. These little feelings of shame or anger or fear or whatever else are important. They are your keys to freedom. If you don't write them down to catch them, they will run away and you may not be able to recall them. Once that happens, they become more suppressed and they grow in power, keeping you enslaved. Writing them down brings them into the light and their power diminishes so that you can be free. So pretty please, with sugar on top, write them down!

The head mess of a nicotine addict goes like this, *"I am experiencing fear, therefore I need to smoke. I am experiencing a down, therefore I need to smoke. I am experiencing tiredness so I need to relax and smoke. I am experiencing a little anxiety about this situation, therefore I need to smoke."*

After every smoke, we still feel fearful, down, tired and anxious.

"I am experiencing feeling secure and comfortable so clearly, I need to smoke. I am experiencing feeling filled after the meal so I need to smoke. I am feeling at peace and well so I need a smoke. I am experiencing feeling satisfied after the sex so I need a smoke."

All these thoughts are just thoughts, but because there are other thoughts of *"I shouldn't smoke"*, *"I am weak"*, *"I am a slave"*, *"it is killing me"*, there is a debate going on. Thoughts create feelings. The debate creates uncomfortable feelings. The only way to be rid of the uncomfortable feelings is to end the debate. Once the decision is made to have a cigarette the uncomfortable feelings disappear because the debate has ended, NOT because of the drug. You feel better instantly, the first inhalation, before the drug has had any chance of getting to your brain. This process is the illusion that makes people think smoking helps you relax. To an addict, every feeling is because of withdrawal and every thought leads to a drug use and therefore having the drug will solve it if not fully, at least partially. It is nonsense. It is insanity.

And then there is 'if'. If I don't have a smoke now, I will be feeling anxious later. If I don't get one in now, I'll feel worse towards the end of the meeting. If I don't smoke two now, I'll feel uncomfortable half way through the whatever.

Open your mind

In this section we will create a way of allowing your mind to accept new possibilities and to accept challenges to your current beliefs. There will be instruction as to how to open your mind; a story about dramatic shifts in beliefs and a revelation of a crucial key to freedom – seeing where you are wrong. By the end of the section you will have been opened to new possibilities and you will have been given the wonderful freedom to change.

The first thing you need to do is open your mind, so that the addiction in your subconscious can be brought into your conscious mind where it can't keep tripping you up. How do we open our minds? We consider the possibility that we might be wrong. We consider the possibility that we might have been quite wrong for a long time. We might even have been stark staringly wrong about this thing all of our lives. We might just be completely and utterly wrong and what's worse - somebody else might be right. Come with me through this story I have to tell.

Imagine you are on a subway train or a bus. At the next stop a man with three children gets on the bus or train. The man sits down and stares out the window looking as if he doesn't have a care in the world. One of his children is running up and down the centre aisle pretending to be a fighter-plane in a battle. The father notices but says nothing. The other boy is laughing and screaming wildly at his brother and it reminds you of a horror film about a mental asylum. The little girl goes from passenger to passenger, staring right into their faces. She comes to you and just stands right in front of your face, staring at you amid all the noise and commotion caused by the other two kids. The father does absolutely nothing. He makes no attempt at all to control his kids in any way. They are his kids and he just lets them run riot. I want you to notice how you are feeling right now in this situation. How are you feeling about this irresponsible father and about the fact that you are being disturbed because he will not parent his kids properly. Picture it. Feel the feelings. Take a while.

The man and his kids were returning home from the hospital where his wife and their mother had just died of cancer right in front of them during the visit. Take a while. Now how do you feel?

Things change not because they necessarily actually change, but because we have just been given a little more information, a little bit of truth or wisdom we hadn't previously known. How you think and feel can change dramatically by a little piece of information. Sometimes a little information about one issue can be the key to freedom for a person. Each of us has certain strong beliefs about smoking that keep us trapped in the addiction. Many of our beliefs are the same, but some are stronger than others and this varies from individual to individual. Quite often, each of us just needs one or two keys for these locked doors in our minds that can open up for us the world of freedom. For example you might have shame or fear about certain smells and finding a way through that may be your main key to freedom from this addiction. For others it will be a different issue or issues.

This course is about getting the information you need to become free from your addiction. You were wrong to think and feel what you were thinking and feeling about the situation above. You were wrong because of your ignorance and fear. Ignorance of the situation and the reasons for that situation, fear that there are parents like that whose neglect is having an uncomfortable effect on your life. You are addicted to cigarettes because of your ignorance and fear. You're not addicted to cigarettes because of the drug. You are addicted to cigarettes because of your ignorance and fear. You think they taste nice, you're wrong. You think you always really want one, you're wrong. You think they help you relax, you're wrong. You think they give you pleasure, you're wrong. Opening your mind means accepting the possibility that you might be wrong and what's even worse, somebody else might be right!

You might . . .

. . . be WRONG?

It's ok to be wrong. It might be that what you currently think and feel and believe about a certain thing is what everyone else thinks too and that makes it right. You're wrong. History is full of examples of whole nations and races being completely and utterly wrong about many, many things. Once you make the decision that you are probably wrong and someone else is probably right, then you have opened your mind and you will finish this course not needing or wanting a cigarette ever again. If you can't make the decision to be wrong then you are wasting your time. I want you to really think about this now and make a decision about it now. I will tell you absolutely and exactly why you are wrong. But if you don't decide now that you are already wrong, then you will be completely unable to hear the alternative explanation about how you are wrong. You would not be reading this if you weren't wrong about something, you would already have stopped smoking by now. Surrender is the key to victory. That is a universal, spiritual truth. It is not logical or understandable, if it was it would probably be wrong.

Looking for where you are wrong is the key to your freedom. Be willing to be wrong and then you will hear and take in and absorb and understand. Defend your position, or try to be right and you will stay stuck in your bunker and freedom will never be yours. Think of it this way. You are on a piece of ground and you are right to be on this piece of ground. You have been on this piece of ground for a long time. Your piece of ground is your knowledge and belief and it is your life. You pick up this course and I attack you on your ground. My attacks on you are intended to move you off your ground to some other ground over there. The other ground over there is unfamiliar, you don't know what it's like so naturally you are anxious and frightened to go there, but worse than that, if you leave the ground you are on you will have to leave all your possessions as well. The possessions are your beliefs that comfort you with certainty and security. It is only natural that you will resist any attacks and you will try to defend yourself. So you build your bunker and defend it at all costs with panic and fear and justification and reason.

But just think for a minute about exactly what you are defending. This particular piece of ground is where you are stuck in your nicotine addiction. It is your prison, the place in which you are the slave. This piece of ground you are defending is not somewhere I or anyone else would want to be. May I suggest to you it is ok to surrender. It is ok to question your beliefs and even to give them up. Throw down your weapons and walk out of your bunker on to the new ground over there. Can it be really worse than the place you are in now?

The truth will set you free

This section is a general overview of the beliefs of nicotine addiction. We will also look at how the addiction operates on a physical as well as psychological level, including some chemical processes that occur in the brain. By the end of the section you will understand the basic mechanics of nicotine addiction and what is meant by 'permanent freedom'.

To be rid of illusion is to know truth. The key to permanent freedom from smoking is the permanent freedom from all the illusions that keep you smoking. You continue to smoke because of your illusions, if you didn't have any illusions you simply would not smoke because you would have absolutely no reason to. If you want to be free from your addiction to smoking, you must know the truth about how cigarettes work, and how they don't work. To demonstrate how cigarettes work I want you to do a simple exercise. First, take a rubber band and entwine it around the fingers of one hand. Stay like that for a little while. This is the point where you haven't had a cig for just a little while and you have just thought about having one. Now you've just made the decision not to have one for a while longer, so make the rubber band tighter around your fingers. Stay like that just for a while. Now you decide you are not going to think about smoking at all so tighten the band even more. Try not to think about the pain. Stay like that for a little while. Now remove the rubber band, breathe in deeply and wiggle your fingers and enjoy their freedom. Feel the relief. Now you feel better and less uncomfortable. If it is relief you are looking for then just keep a rubber band handy at all times. It's cheaper and healthier than smoking. You don't really need to do this exercise with the rubber band to know that if you set up some pain, then you will derive pleasure when you relieve that pain. That is all smoking really is.

This is how the addiction works. The very first cigarette you had put nicotine in your brain. The nicotine left your brain shortly afterwards and the feeling of the drug leaving your brain is like a feeling of emptiness, something missing that you can't quite put your finger on, a feeling a bit like hunger. Then you feel a little anxious and you begin to panic. Then you have a panic attack until you realise that all you have to do is to replace the nicotine and you will feel filled again. Filling yourself again feels like relief from pain. The first cigarette created the first craving and every cigarette you have ever had since has been to get relief from this craving. It's like pinching yourself to get pain in order to feel the relief of not pinching yourself.

So why does the drug nicotine create so much craving, fear and panic? Well the answer is - it doesn't. It is an illusion. When you smoke, nicotine enters your bloodstream through the lung walls. When the nicotine in your blood gets to your brain it comes into contact with receptors that accommodate the shape of the nicotine molecules, so the nicotine sticks. The receptors are not an exact match so the nicotine molecules don't have a very good grip so within about ten minutes the blood washes away the nicotine molecules. The nicotine leaves your brain and your brain notices it has gone. On the sub-conscious level - something that was there, is now gone. This is noticed so easily because it goes quite quickly - within an hour half of it is gone. It is this speed at which it leaves your brain that is important. If it left slowly and gradually it wouldn't be noticed and there would be no addiction. But because it leaves quite quickly, it is noticed. There is no need to get all technical and scientific and identify which particular receptors in which particular area of the brain the nicotine molecules latch on to. The point is, after a while their weak bond is broken and the blood washes them away and out of the system. The point is they leave quite quickly and it is noticed.

When a human being is deprived of something while looking away at the time, there are feelings of surprise, shock, loss, betrayal, grief, disbelief, anger, anxiety, insecurity, fear, sadness, longing, panic. All these feelings exist because we are complex creatures with complex brains living in a complex world. When your conscious mind feels the sub-conscious loss it searches for the answer and somehow it knows that replacing the nicotine will cure the sense of loss. The reason we think we can easily stop smoking when we first start is because the conscious mind hasn't yet really got used to the idea that these feelings are due to a drug leaving the brain rather quickly. So the conscious mind looks for other answers and it finds them. We have all suffered loss of some sort. This sub-conscious feeling or loss is bound to remind us of genuine loss, genuine grief, sadness, loneliness, anger, anxiety, fear etc. So what has happened is that this slight loss has connected with much deeper and bigger feelings about real unresolved issues that we don't want to, or simply can't yet deal with. This is what happens when you suddenly discover you have lost some paper cash from your pocket. It's no great loss but the feelings are connecting to greater and deeper losses. So initially, the slight sense of loss that is detected by the sub-conscious mind translates into the conscious mind as being depressed, or feeling low or insecure probably because of all the reasons we have generally felt like that. Initially we don't connect that feeling with nicotine loss. This slight feeling passes quite unnoticed if we don't then smoke another cigarette. However, if we do, we feel a sense of relief from the loss we hadn't noticed we were feeling before. Instead of being aware that we are just being relieved from the sense of loss we had when the last load of nicotine left we translate this feeling into beliefs that cigarettes are changing how we feel – i.e. they help us relax etc.

The feeling of pleasure you get when you smoke is a feeling of relief, like taking off the rubber band. That explains why you get more pleasure from smoking after a period of enforced deprivation when you can't smoke for a while such as after a bus journey or a flight or after a meal or exercise session or sex. The longer you have to wait, the greater the relief. The leaving of the nicotine from the brain sets off a chain reaction that tricks us into believing we need another cigarette.

There is another reason we believe we need another cigarette - because we have been taught that it is true. We have seen thousands of people thousands of times on TV, in films, at home and work, light up a cigarette and be relieved from the way they are feeling. This belief is not questioned. The illusion is that a cigarette does much more than simply replaces the nicotine that was there from the last cigarette. Our belief that the cigarette will change the way we feel ensures that we keep the current uncomfortable feelings **until** we have another cigarette. The genuine initial slight feeling created when nicotine goes from our brain is easy for us to cope with. We can easily deal with the empty feeling because we know that we will be able to have a smoke during the next break. It is only when we realise that we are the only smoker and we have run out of cigarettes and there are no shops nearby that the panic and fear comes along, and all the insane schemes arise to make enough excuses to go to any lengths to find a cigarette. Patches don't work for so many because it's the belief that drives the panic - not the lack of nicotine.

The vast majority of the time we don't know that all this subconscious stuff is going on, we just think, "I want a cig". It's only when we try stopping, or are not allowed to smoke that the fear and panic comes - and even then we haven't a clue what is going on or why, so we blame the drug or 'withdrawals', in our ignorance and fear.

All this happens in the brain. Our muscles, heart, lungs, liver, kidneys, hands, shoulders, feet and toes don't miss or notice any lack of nicotine. They don't even notice the increased oxygen after the nicotine and carbon dioxide is gone. There are physical sensations when withdrawing, but these are brought on by the panic attack and ensuing adrenaline rush.

Addiction is a constant pulling of withdrawal and relief, withdrawal and relief. You get up out of bed and you are withdrawing, so you smoke and get relief. One is never enough so you smoke some more. After breakfast you are withdrawing so you get some relief, coffee and a smoke. You get in the car and after a short while being on the road the nicotine is leaving you so you light another cigarette. You light another cigarette because you know that if you don't, you will suffer withdrawals soon (that feeling of emptiness and being a little uncomfortable). You can't smoke on the bus so you sit on the bus and accept it. You don't suffer because you know that you will be able to have a cigarette when you get off the bus. You don't suffer with the withdrawal sensation because it is such a slight feeling anyway, hardly noticeable. You've had the withdrawals all night, but without your conscious mind with its beliefs, it is such a slight feeling it didn't even wake you. But when you get off the bus you suddenly start suffering, why, because the real suffering is all in your mind, it is what you believe, therefore it is. Whatever and however your story goes, your life is one of addiction, a constant pulling of withdrawal and relief, withdrawal and relief ad infinitum. This goes on and on and on and that is your life

AND IT IS UNACCEPTABLE!!!!

It is unacceptable to you to do that to yourself.

If the nicotine didn't stick to any bits in the brain, there would be no addiction and no problem. You would simply put the cigarette out and that would be the end of that particular experience and your conscious mind would wonder why on earth you did that to yourself and you probably would never do it again. After all, there was no pleasure had, it tasted foul and it didn't even get you high. If the nicotine clung to the bits in the brain really well and left the system very gradually over a couple of days or so there would be no problem. The nicotine leaving would not be noticed, there wouldn't be a feeling of something missing all of a sudden and there would be no fear or anxiety or panic. The fact that the nicotine clings on for a while after the cigarette has been put out then most of it leaves at once after a short time, means the loss is sensed and there is anxiety about the loss, this leads to panic and adrenaline and we call this withdrawal. Our conscious minds can and already do over-ride withdrawal. This is why people are able to break free. Our conscious minds, with their beliefs actually create most of what we call withdrawal, beliefs of pleasure and need and help and use. Because of this, our conscious minds can also over-ride actual physical withdrawal very easily.

Firstly, if physical withdrawal was in any way particularly uncomfortable, a smoker could never get a night's sleep. Would you ask a heroin addict to sleep through his withdrawals? Of course not!

So actual physical withdrawal from nicotine is so slight, if indeed it exists at all, it doesn't even wake us from our sleep. Get a good grasp of this truth. Physical withdrawal from nicotine is virtually non existent. At most it creates a slight sense of loss that couldn't last more than a few minutes on its own. It's our conscious minds with their fears and memories and experiences and unreal beliefs that turns this very slight and very temporary sense of loss into the madness and insanity that accompanies every decision to stop or cut down a little. So because it is our conscious minds that create the difficulties, it is only our conscious minds that can set us free. Once we are free on a conscious level, the object of this course, we can then experience the initial slight sense of loss around ten or twenty minutes after we put out our last cigarette for the few minutes it lasts, and that would be the end of the matter. Our conscious minds can override the desire and need and panic attack, simply by being conscious of the truth when it runs out of all the mistaken beliefs. The other, and for our purposes, more important reason we know that our conscious minds create all this head mess and can therefore easily over-ride it, is an experience just about every smoker has already had.

When I became free from my head mess, people noticed I wasn't smoking any more and they also noticed it wasn't bothering me at all; in fact my life and health and attitude had improved a great deal from negative to positive. One fella in particular said to me that he knew it wasn't the drug that was the problem because he had just been on holiday to Australia, and he couldn't smoke for ten hours. He said that during the flight he didn't suffer withdrawals or anything and in fact he didn't think about smoking and he was fine with that. Then he said that when he got off the plane and into the airport he decided he might as well not bother smoking any more, because clearly, he didn't need to and like all smokers the truth is he always wanted to be free. He was fine getting through customs and the airport itself. As soon as he got outside the Airport he experienced a compelling urge to smoke over which he was powerless, so he smoked and that was the end of that. But during the flight, not smoking didn't bother him at all. It is easy to see from this experience that so called withdrawal is not physical it is psychological. It is also not difficult to work out that what is going on in the subconscious can be easily over-ridden by the conscious mind when it knows there is no point in entertaining any beliefs of pleasure or need or desperate withdrawal because there simply cannot be any smoking right now so we might as well accept it. Once that bloke made a decision in the airport to not smoke any more, all the issues in the conscious and sub-conscious mind started having an argument. No part of his mind really knew that smoking wasn't a pleasure or a help or a need and it agreed that stopping was very difficult because of the tremendous physical withdrawal so why ruin a once in a lifetime holiday suffering in this way? And that was the end of that matter. Can you see this is all head mess; it's got nothing to do with the drug! It's got nothing to do with willpower. It's got nothing to do with internal chemicals or genes or biology.

Now think back to a time, apart from every single night when you sleep, when you have gone for a long period of time not being able to smoke and not suffering particularly as a result. Any public transport is a good example because there is now no smoking on most buses and trains and coaches and all planes. A major factor to consider is that when we are put in these situations, we accept it and don't really suffer because we know we will be smoking later. There is no debate going on in our minds about levels of suffering we may endure or missing out on any pleasure or having any need. So how do we stay on that plane or coach or train? We deal with the debate. We deal with the issues. We make a decision about all these things now so that there is nothing to debate about it again. We decide there is no pleasure, they don't taste nice, there is no need and being free is a pleasure not a difficulty. We make these decisions based on truth and that is the end of the matter. There is never again any need to have a debate about the decisions we are making right now because we have learned the truth of the matter. There is no longer any debate so there simply are no withdrawals. If indeed any panic or fear comes up out of sheer habit, that is simply an opportunity to reinforce our new true beliefs and the panic and fear will leave us. Eventually, after a very short time period, that panic and fear can never come back because there are no issues or arguments to debate over.

Mostly, when that panic and fear comes along, we presume that there is some chemical interaction with the addictive drug going on that creates those feelings. This is simply not true. We are wrong. What is actually happening is a sub-conscious debate going on regarding the need and pleasure set against the panic and pain, and we always lose this debate. Now we bring this debate out of our sub-conscious and into our conscious minds. We look at all the issues of pleasure, need, pain and fear and all the beliefs connected to these feelings and we deal with them consciously. We make decisions about them once and for all until there are no issues left to debate.

If it is true that our belief creates craving and withdrawals, then why hasn't someone mentioned this before? Even people who have never smoked believe that smoking is pleasurable and provides relief from stress and ends the craving and withdrawals. Non-smokers are smart enough not to smoke at all but even they have these beliefs and even they think they may be missing out on something. They don't do it because they can see that the price for that bit of pleasure is too great and can't possibly be worth it.

The only pleasure is relief from the withdrawal the last cigarette created. There is no other pleasure.

Addiction?

Is nicotine addictive? If you read up on scientific reports about nicotine addiction you will find a mish-mash of conflicting nonsense. Some respected scientists have even found a gene responsible for nicotine addiction, claiming that is the reason some people smoke and some don't. Apparently there is also an 'evil' gene and a criminal behaviour gene. Some scientists use withdrawal symptoms as a marker to prove that nicotine is an addictive substance. They overlook the fact that fear produces adrenaline which produces these physical symptoms. They then go on to explain that nicotine is psychoactive like heroin. Let me assure you here and now that nicotine is in no way anything like as psychoactive as heroin, in fact the only psychoactive element to smoking is the carbon monoxide which makes you feel a bit dizzy. After a while our beliefs translate this dizziness into being a stimulating pleasure. To be fair to the scientists, the brain is bound to have reactions to the sudden onslaught of toxic substances, so naturally it is going to produce some dopamine, but this isn't anything like the stimulating pleasure you get from something like heroin and the small level of dopamine the brain produces could in no way be 'felt' as a stimulating pleasure.

If the drug nicotine was addictive, then everyone who stopped smoking would suffer withdrawals. The fact is that millions of people have stopped smoking, and millions of them just stopped one day and suffered little or no withdrawals whatsoever. The only scientific explanation of this fact is that there must be a nicotine gene which predisposes some people to suffer withdrawal and some people not. Ridiculous. I am a smoker who suffered withdrawal of horrendous proportions many, many times. But when I was freed from my illusions the withdrawals miraculously disappeared. Maybe that gene co-incidentally was not working properly any more, just when I became free from my illusions. I'm afraid the truth is that scientists do not have any clue whatsoever about addiction. They do not understand that the power of addiction lies in psychological fear, not what the drug does. I can absolutely assure you here and now that the vast majority of people who have got clean from heroin addiction found that a lot easier than stopping smoking. What the drug does plays a relatively small part in addiction. Another addiction that is as dangerous and prevalent as smoking is overeating. Food addiction has got nothing to do with the psychoactive effect of cheesy quavers. In exactly the same way, nicotine addiction has got nothing to do with the psychoactive effects of filter tipped.

Food addiction, heroin addiction and cigarette addiction are all about filling the emptiness. They try to satisfy a powerful hunger that cannot be satisfied. There are books and reports and theses and opinions aplenty on the nature of the hunger that cannot be satisfied, or the emptiness inside that cannot be filled, or the spiritual void of the inner self that is as boundary-less as a child. Even though this is the central cause of addiction, it is not going to be the subject of serious investigation in this book. This is because it is a highly complex subject and to tackle that emptiness on a personal level requires the commitment of a lifetime. However, to ignore this central core of addiction would render this course incomplete and leave a gap in our understanding, so we will look a little at this part of us that is the addiction.

There are many means and way of viewing the emptiness inside. We could use a spiritual view or psychological view. One tried and tested method is to view the emptiness as an inner child that is never satisfied. Opening up a communication with this inner child is an effective way to deal with the empty feeling. The inner child is the hunger. Your inner child is hungry for love and attention and comfort. This child is the addiction. The question then is, do we have to be in touch with this inner child in order to be free from nicotine addiction? The answer is no. So why mention it? Because I want you to be aware that addiction is a psychological hunger that cannot be filled. Once you know that it cannot be filled you can choose not to try to fill it. You can see that hunger or addiction or craving as being that part of you that is seeking love and fulfilment, God or comfort or security. The part of you that seeks being filled and satisfied through drugs, work, money, sex, religion, relationships, gambling or food. It is there for a purpose, so that you would know your heart's secrets, but it is complex and it cannot be satisfied by one cigarette or two or ten or twenty, a hundred, a thousand or a million.

Dopamine

When you smoke a cigarette your brain produces a chemical called dopamine. Your system is under attack from poisonous fumes so your brain has evolved to help you cope with attacks by producing chemicals that will help you fight. One of these is adrenaline the other is dopamine. Dopamine is like morphine in that it makes you feel good and has some anaesthetic value. When you experience the effect of morphine or dopamine and then it is washed out of your system there can be a bit of a come down. This contributes to what we refer to as withdrawals. The wearing off of the dopamine creates a concern, a little bit of anxiety and this anxiety creates a little adrenaline. If you enjoy the experience of taking a drug that stimulates dopamine production then there are better drugs you could use. Nicotine is relatively inefficient at doing this because it is the fact that you are under attack from poisons that stimulates the dopamine, not the nicotine itself. Either way, it doesn't stimulate enough for you to notice, if it did you would get high and you don't get high. Cigarettes do nothing for you at all except they seem to relieve the symptoms of withdrawal the last cigarette created. They don't relieve anything of course; those so-called withdrawal symptoms will pass whether you smoke or not.

Adrenaline

When you have some anxiety or fear or shock, your body goes into fight or flight mode. It prepares you chemically to have a fight or to run away. It does this by stimulating the pineal gland

52

to produce adrenaline. My Brother used to be a police officer and he told me that despite what you see on TV, when a criminal is running from the police it is very rare they are caught because they are pumped up with adrenaline so they can run faster and jump higher and be incredibly strong. This is what adrenaline gives you, super strength and speed. The stories are legion of acts of great, superhuman feats of strength when people are saving someone's life or protecting their young or saving their own lives.

Someone once wrote a book in which the author describes an experience he had that demonstrates the power of adrenaline. Adrenaline is a very powerful drug which the body produces naturally. This person acquired a small vial of adrenaline. It has to be taken from live donors, but because it is so powerful it goes a very long way. He put a matchstick into the vial of adrenaline and then put that very tiny drop of adrenaline on the end of the match on to his tongue. He immediately went into involuntary convulsions followed by seizure.

Have you ever seen the film 'Pulp Fiction'? Well, in one scene of the film this girl has taken a heroin overdose and she is clearly dying, and she has fallen into a deep coma. The hero then gives her a shot of adrenaline into her heart and it jolts her out of the coma instantly. Although this is only a film, that is how adrenaline works, immediate and dramatic.

So what produces adrenaline? Fear, shock, anxiety, panic. What produces these feelings? – a thought – conscious or subconscious. A tiny, microscopic, but steady release of adrenaline will produce physical feelings of discomfort, tension, tightness, cramps, itchiness, heat, constipation even nausea. This is what withdrawing addicts experience. The physical sensations

53

themselves create thoughts and feeling of fear and anxiety and it can become a self perpetuating cycle of fear and panic.

That's why addicts who decide to quit go nuts over absolutely nothing at all. None of this has got anything to do with the actual drug they are not having. It's entirely to do with what they believe they are missing out on, the fear of the absence of the crutch.

Because adrenaline is such a powerful drug, the body and mind have certain safety systems so that you don't die from adrenaline overdose. You have a guarantee. No-one ever died, or has been damaged in any way by nicotine withdrawal. Once your mind feels safe without the drug the fear goes, the adrenaline is not produced and the physical reaction goes. Every single person who has stopped smoking does not suffer physical discomfort for long. The only reason they suffer in the first place is because of the lies they believe. Many, many smokers who have quit never suffered at all.

These are facts. This is the truth. There is no such thing as nicotine withdrawal. When a person makes a decision to not smoke they have a belief they are missing out on some familiar pleasure or security and this creates anxiety, fear then panic. An extremely slight production of adrenaline is stimulated which creates a little unfamiliar (therefore discomforting) physical sensation. This creates anxiety, fear and panic. On and on this cycle goes and before long you go nuts so you smoke. The nicotine does nothing whatsoever but you believe it will help so the fear and the panic goes away. You only have to cope with the obnoxious fumes instead, but that's ok because it's familiar, because you believe it is helping you in some way and the truth is you are insane because of your ignorance of what is really happening. If you have ever experienced this adrenaline cycle and thought it was because you needed to smoke, remember that as soon as you made the decision to smoke again, most of the uncomfortable feelings were relieved before any cigarette went near your mouth. The decision solved the withdrawal NOT the nicotine.

Now you know why you feel the way you feel and you know to ask the question, *what is the thought behind the feeling?* you will find you will not be afraid and you will not suffer in any physical way. You are free. You can look every thought and feeling squarely in the face and your knowledge and awareness of these processes has already taken away the fear and uncertainty. You are free for life.

Image

In this section we will look at how advertisers' images, images we see in films and television, and self-image affect nicotine addiction. By the end of the section you will be able to identify how these images have affected you and how they can continue to affect your addiction to nicotine so that you are free from their sub-conscious grip.

Smoking has an image. In fact, like most things, it has several images. In days gone by the image advertisers tried to put across was that smoking was a grown up thing to do and it helped you relax and deal with stress. Smoking meant you were accepted as an adult and would be taken seriously. Smoking was connected to heroism and sex and being cool. In films the stars smoked which made smoking not just acceptable but cool. If you didn't smoke there was a perceived risk of not being accepted in the gang. You risked being thought of as a wimp. This concept is as alive today as it has always been. It is still part of our culture. One of the reasons I started smoking was to prove something to my mates who did smoke. It was like a rite of passage. This still happens in hundreds of bike sheds behind hundreds of schools today.

Films and television, despite government bans, do portray smoking illusions such as it helps you relax, concentrate etc. The main thing they do however is to make smoking look cool. Our heroes and heroines smoke and this is a loveable flaw in their basic characters. Heroes tend not to be without serious flaws because if they were good and clean people they wouldn't find themselves extreme dysfunctional situations that make for such good drama and film. We don't like males who are pretty and clean and we don't like women who wear sensible shoes. They are not heroes. Now here is the point – you just would not believe how powerful these images of our heroes are to our subconscious personalities. Even if you work through all the illusions about smoking there can still be this slight draw from deep within because somewhere in our minds is the picture of one of our heroes smoking in a particular situation in a film. It is a difficult image to let go of because it feels like we are giving up our coolness. Our egos do not want to let go of this image. Can you think of your ego's image of the hero who is smoking? See if you can bring it to mind now, just take a moment to try and find any image that might be inside of a film character smoking and being cool. Most of us do have such an image inside of us. If you can't find yours right now then maybe you don't have one or maybe it will come up later. Either way, when you have brought this image to your conscious mind you will notice that the thought of not smoking becomes somewhat frightening or at least, you experience a little anxiety, a little panic attack. This is your ego not wanting to let go of the hero or heroes because they will no longer be such heroes if you let go of smoking or because you will lose the acceptance of those people if you become a sensible non-smoker with no real problem about it one way or the other. Your connection to them will seem severed. In reality you don't have any connection to those fictional characters at all whether you smoke or not, but in your mind there is something there. All I suggest to you is that whether real or not, it is there and behind the thought that you may not be accepted by your heroes because you no longer smoke is a feeling of fear and panic at the threat of rejection. It is just a feeling to be aware of.

Now that you are aware of it, it can no longer cause the panic it would have done when you had no idea at all why you were feeling what you were feeling. It is a thought and a feeling to look out for so that you do not become its victim the next time round.

For many years advertisers have tried to influence people to smoke by making it cool, or manly. The tobacco industry has spent billions. This may, or may not, encourage people to smoke. You see, I don't know whether or not the advertising is effective. There are millions of people who smoke cannabis, are hooked on tranquillisers and you don't see many adverts about spliffs or tamazis. However, the advertising has put into our culture these beliefs of smoking being cool or mature. These beliefs have been successfully implanted into our brains whether we like to admit it or not. Nobody today really believes it is cool or grown-up to smoke, in a conscious way, but sub-consciously, these notions do exist. Smoking, for the most part, doesn't appear on television or in films any more, but think about why you first chose to smoke. Did you do it to prove something, to be accepted, to fit in?

During the latter years of my smoking, I actually became embarrassed that I was in the minority. I was the one with the dirty habit, the one who was causing the smell and the coughing, the one who had to hang around outside. I felt embarrassed that I was trapped in this negative unsociable slavery. It is not longer the fashionable, cool, respected thing to do. It has become socially unacceptable.

So advertising creates images and beliefs we don't really believe or we have grown out of. Our culture really does know it isn't cool or mature; in fact, it's a sign of weakness and lack of will-power. Smoking today has a very negative image and this attracts millions of young people rebelling against authority. It still makes smoking cool for many youngsters. OK, so maybe this is not just the advertisers fault, so what do the advertisers do now?

It is important to be aware, just in case there are any sub-conscious beliefs in you that an advert could trigger off as a reason or excuse to smoke. Some advertisers make it sophisticated, some funny, some work on fear.

Adverts that try to uphold an image of sophistication use beautiful models in beautiful locations, or they use art, particularly modern art. Some tobacco companies produce some wonderful images in a very glossy, intelligent and sophisticated way. Some adverts try to be funny. A more interesting development in recent years has been the fear trigger adverts. These adverts are designed to increase the fear and disgust of smoking. The more you can disgust and make fearful a drug addict, the more the need to feel better is increased and to have more of the drug. Addiction is all about fear. The more fear and self disgust there is, the more trapped is the addict. So some cigarette adverts have negative, disturbing, grotesque images that have connotations of dirtiness, sickness and death. I remember seeing a poster that used an old marriage saying: something old, something new, something borrowed, something blue. The first image, something old, was an object that looked yellowed by nicotine smoke rather than age, it was exactly that colour. This is to remind a smoker that he looks older and dirtier because he smokes. The second image, something new, was of an insect. It was not like any insect you had seen before; it was a new insect with red bits and a fierce looking pointy stinger at the front and was clearly a killer. This is to remind the smoker that smoking is dangerous and it kills people. The third image, something borrowed, was of a box of dental floss, to remind the smoker that it would only ever be a borrowed item because it is useless to a dirty smoker with yellow teeth to own such a thing. So after three images of dirtiness, early ageing, death, yellow teeth then there is something blue – the ribbon design on a packet of cigarettes. Because after being disturbed, frightened and disgusted by the previous three grotesque images you really do need another cig right now.

The point is that advertising, whether by tobacco companies or government health campaigns, can trigger fears, beliefs and connotations of image and original motives for smoking. Where did that last trigger of fear come from? - I just saw an advert and that's all there is to it. I am free!

Now please say out loud six times – just do it!

__These__ feelings and this confusion will pass whether I smoke or not.
These feelings and this confusion __will__ pass whether I smoke or not.
These feelings and this confusion will __pass__ whether I smoke or not.
These feelings and this confusion will pass __whether__ I smoke or not.
These feelings and this confusion will pass whether __I__ smoke or not.
These feelings and this confusion will pass whether I smoke __or not__.

Self Image

The issue about image is not merely an important issue in terms of advertising; it is also very important with regard to self image. The image you hold inside yourself about yourself affects your whole life. There are many books out today that deal with your own self image, your own internal messages regarding what you believe about yourself and life generally. Are your thoughts about yourself positive and accepting and nurturing, or are they negative, judgemental and self-defeating? Smoking can quite literally be an expression of habitual negative thoughts and beliefs about yourself. If your bottom line is, *"I am not good enough"* then certainly the act of smoking will support and comfort you in that belief.

We have already seen how advertisers can use the self-disgust and fear that accompanies any addiction. It is like a Catch 22 situation. The more fear and disgust you feel about the addiction, the greater your need for comfort, and the stronger the addiction becomes. The stronger the addiction becomes, the more fear and self-disgust you have, the greater is your need for comfort and the stronger the addiction becomes. That is why it is difficult to look at the issues and beliefs about smoking, the very thoughts that keep you trapped, while you are trying to stop smoking. It is much easier to look at all the issues and illusions about the addiction while you are still smoking because you are not panicking and being fearful and needy.

So, what if your smoking is a reflection of your own poor self-image? An expression of your own internal belief that you are not good enough, not worth it? Then surely until that changes there is nothing you can do about the actual addiction, because the addiction is a result of something else inside. *'There is nothing can be done about the addiction until you change that negative self-image inside'*. This thought can keep an addict trapped in the addiction for a lifetime. It is true that having a negative self-image or low self-esteem is certainly a powerful element of the complex nature of addiction, however it is less true of smoking than other addictions. Smoking has no actual physical effect. It does not make you feel better. Certainly if you were to imbibe in a few beers, a big spliff or a dig of charlie your feelings would be changed and you would undoubtedly feel better than you did - in the short-term. However a cigarette is not going to change your feelings for you in any way whatsoever. Smoking is actually rather an inefficient expression of negative self-beliefs. It is a poor substitute for a serious drug problem or gambling problem or an exciting range of weirdo perverted sex obsessions one could choose. But nevertheless, it is an addiction and therefore is likely to be an expression of some negative self-beliefs all be it that it may well be only a week negative belief. The main expression of self-disgust that smoking reflects is the fact that you are a smoker. The negative self image is that you are a trapped, enslaved addict. You don't need a more serious negative self belief than that to feed the nicotine addiction. The nicotine addiction is simply an expression of the self-disgust a nicotine addict feels for being a nicotine addict in the first place.

You might think that this is not sufficient explanation because at the end of the day, anyone who poisons themselves that many times a day every day of their lives can't possible have any self-love or self-respect or self-esteem. It doesn't work like that. This is something you cannot quantify. You can't make a measure of negative self-belief from a measure of an addiction. Remember, you probably didn't start smoking to feel better, you started out of curiosity and simply wanting to fit in and prove yourself. Initially, starting smoking was not an expression of negative self-belief, it was actually an expression of courage and self confidence because you were going to prove that you wouldn't get addicted. So when you began it was an expression of positives. You were not trying to feel better you were trying to expand and explore. The only negative self-disgust you have is that you were duped by the complex set of illusions that make up this addiction, just like millions of other people are. The self-disgust that you think may be an expression of negative self-beliefs is purely and simply the self-disgust you feel about being a smoker. Nicotine addiction creates its own self-disgust that keeps you addicted. You do not need to connect this self-disgust you have about smoking to any internal negative self-beliefs because the two are not connected and did not originate in the first place in any connected way.

Nevertheless, even when you began smoking you knew it was highly addictive. If you felt you had something to prove that must indicate some lack of self-esteem in the first place. Therefore smoking is an expression of negative self-beliefs even though it is admittedly an indirect expression.

There is a slight flaw in this theory. Might it be possible that you are changing the negatives inside? The fact that you are reading this book today may be a reflection of a goal to change, working from your positive beliefs and thoughts. You have made the effort and spent the money and committed yourself to reading this book today. So you do have enough self-esteem and self respect to face and deal with this self-defeating behaviour. Everyone has a balance of negative and positive thoughts and beliefs about themselves and about life. Everyone who is still alive, still surviving this world has enough positive thoughts to continue to live. There are many whose negative thoughts and beliefs make it impossible for them to carry on living. But for you who are reading this book today, you not only have enough

63

positives to survive, you also have enough to make the effort to get free from this self defeating behaviour. You have enough self-respect and courage to confront and face your illusions and to have your beliefs challenged. You already have enough self-love and devotion to . . . change. Change for the better. Change as an act of love and courage and commitment. This needs saying because its true. Clearly, you are good enough, you are worth this. If you really didn't think so you wouldn't be doing this right now.

You have chosen to open a scary book you've never seen before to read the thoughts of someone you don't know who is going to tell you for the next few hours how very wrong you are about so many things you believe, and you have even paid money for the privilege of putting yourself through all this. Why on earth is that? It can only mean that you care so much about yourself and you have enough honesty and humility to accept that you need help and you trust yourself enough to see this thing through. You are truly tremendous. This is how you can defeat the circle of addiction. When you are feeling negative about yourself, instead of trying to comfort yourself with a negative behaviour you encourage and support yourself by respecting yourself enough by trying and caring.

Do it for yourself

In this section we will look at how misguided motivations to stop smoking are counter-productive and the reasons why we have these motivations. By the end of the section you will know for certain how and why there can only be the one successful motivation.

One of the things that keep countless addicts trapped in their addictions is that they set out to get free from their addiction because of somebody else. Just as most smokers started smoking because somebody else put un-stated pressure on them through teenage peer groups, so many smokers try to stop smoking because of their bosses, partners or kids. I am stopping smoking for them they say. There are two major aspects to this mistake. Firstly, by doing it for somebody else you are not dealing with the issues and illusions regarding smoking. In fact you are increasing the sense of loss and sacrifice that forms part of the addiction anyway because not only are you missing out on something you want, you are missing out because of somebody else. This form of self-sacrifice in itself increases the sense of loss and feeds the illusions of pleasure associated with smoking. The more there is a sense of loss, the more powerful becomes the illusion of pleasure.

Secondly, some people choose to give up for somebody else because of a self-esteem issue. If you have little self worth you might find that you cannot put up with the fear and anxiety caused by deciding to stop smoking unless you are doing it for someone else. Someone who you feel is worth it. If you have a poor sense of self worth you can still become free. All you have to do is to decide to do it for you because you are worth it. This will not solve your basic lack of self-esteem, but you don't have to do that to become free, you just have to make sure that you are not doing it for somebody else and the work you are doing today takes care of the rest of the illusions so that there is not the fear of breaking free that you had before anyway.

It may not necessarily be a self-esteem issue. It may just be a reflection of the very common human trait that it often feels much easier to love someone else than ourselves. We easily find the motivation to go further or work harder in order to meet other people's, especially family, needs.

Another problem with this mistake is that the 'somebody else' in question tends to be other human beings. I have not heard of anyone giving up smoking because of their dog or their car. It's usually another person. People being as reliable as people can be means that the somebody else ends up letting you down. People leave you, bosses sack you or move away, partners leave you or die, kids grow up or die. The reason you've been missing out on your pleasure is now no longer there and the inevitable result is that you stop this reasonless sacrifice and end up smoking again. The people you give up for don't even need to leave you, they just need to let you down and now you have a good reason to smoke again, to get back at them. Usually, the people that a smoker chooses to stop for are people who are bound to let them down because we all let each other down from time to time, particularly those we love.

Some smokers who cannot give up for themselves, give up for God. Sometimes this works. Faith can move mountains and certainly having deep spiritual beliefs can be motivation enough to stop smoking. This way has worked for a great many people.

This way has also failed for a great many people. The reason it fails is the same reason it fails when a smoker tries to stop for somebody else. They do not look at the illusions that make up the addiction and the self-sacrifice can only increase the sense of loss and missing out on a pleasure. God doesn't let people down, but people lose faith and when this happens the reason for not smoking and all that self-sacrifice is now gone. People who don't lose faith can still fail to stop smoking. Maybe it's not the lack of faith in God that is to blame, but the enormous faith in the illusions that make up addiction.

The bottom line is that it is pointless to give up smoking for someone else. Do it for you. You are worth it and you can do it. We don't have to give a list of reasons why we are doing this. We just have to become aware of the reasons we do smoke. That's what reading this book is about. Knowing why you smoke will take away the power of the addiction and give you a choice. If you have awareness about all the illusions about smoking you would never choose to smoke because it is simply something you would not want to do and not doing it is absolutely no problem at all. It's got nothing to do with anyone else.

This is not a good time

In this section we will be looking at a major problem that arises every time the decision is made to stop smoking. We will work through the thoughts and the hidden messages behind those thoughts that keep us trapped in the addiction. By the end of the section you will have no doubt about when is the best time and the only realistic time to stop smoking.

I'll stop when I'm over this patch.

I'll give up when I'm in a better situation.

These thoughts can still affect you when you have stopped smoking, because they can translate into other thought paths.

"This is not a good time" can translate into, *"There will be a better time in the future"*.

"I'll stop when I'm over this patch" can translate into, *"I can't cope right now with not smoking"*

"I'll give up when I'm in a better situation" can translate into, *"I can't stay smoke free while I'm in **this** situation"*

All these thoughts are about a fairyland time in the future when it will be a good time and there will be no patches to get over and you will magically have no situations going on. These thoughts can come at you in the present, in the near future and in the distant future, so we have to look at them in each space. Also, it is important to be aware that such thoughts are powerful and they only come on in times of stress and struggle. When everything is OK you won't hear from them.

What makes these thoughts so powerful? Their power lies in their ability to offer a seemingly reasonable alternative solution and they stay hidden and unresolved until you are defenceless against them. Let's deal with the latter point first.

When you are happy smoking or perhaps miserably smoking but choosing to do nothing about it today, these thoughts do not come up. They are hidden in the background somewhere, comforting and reassuring you, and keeping you chained to the ball of addiction. How are they comforting you? Behind all these thoughts of, "*This isn't a good time right now*", there is an almost sub-conscious comforting reassurance that says, "*It's OK, we'll deal with this another time in the future – i.e. tomorrow. We won't wait until it's too late; we'll beat this just in time*". In time for what? Why lung cancer, throat cancer, stroke, emphysema, heart disease and thrombosis of course. Countless thousands have suffered and died because of these comforting and reassuring thoughts. When it really is too late and an addict does contract emphysema, a new thought takes over. "*Well it's too late now, there's no point*". That's why smokers who have suffered a heart attack still continue to smoke.

This background reassurance is the single most powerful thought that keeps an addict in their addiction. It sounds so sensible and grown up.

"Well really, there's a time and a place for all things you know, after all, you have to think of others and the stress you put them through

69

and they need you right now so don't be so selfish and anyway if you don't finish that other business you might get the sack or at least lose a chance of promotion and what about your family and really at the end of the day, being sensible, you don't have to do this right now, perhaps it would be best if you went away for a week, then you could come back and surprise everybody and everybody will be pleased with you and they'll be patting you on the back except for so-and-so who doesn't like you, ha ha it'll really tick him off, but that's his business he needs to sort himself out, that nice new office clerk might go out with you now you don't smoke and at least going away for a while will spare your family, friend and work colleagues the worst of your withdrawals . . . "

And on and on it goes promising you the earth if you choose not to tackle this issue right now. One reason it is so powerful is because it sounds like the voice of reason. It offers time out of the panic that began when you decided not to smoke. It sounds like the sensible voice of mediation, like a teacher, like a parent. A parent's voice is the most powerful voice in our minds. It may not sound like one of your actual parents. It is the voice of what some psychologists call your own internal critical parent that formed in your mind between the ages of seven and nine. It sounds like your own internal voice of parental authority and love, so you are reassured that the insanity it is feeding you actually has some credence.

It does seem sensible to allocate some time to going through withdrawal so that it doesn't affect your family and work and friends etc. Also, if you take away other stresses like family and work etc; you then have only the stress of withdrawal to cope with. Unfortunately there are several basic flaws to this logic.

You can't allocate time to NOT doing something no matter how long a break you take from life, you have to go back sometime and deal with the issues. Taking time to focus on something that doesn't actually exist is bound to drive you nuts and is unlikely to work.

Several of my smoking friends have gone into hospital and were not allowed to smoke for a short time. As they had not consciously made the decision to stop smoking, they found to their surprise that not smoking was no big deal really, so they decided to stop. Once they had made the decision to stop they experienced a little doubt and anxiety, but they didn't really find it difficult while they were in hospital. As soon as they came out however, they started smoking again. All they had done was experience some truth - there is no such thing as physical withdrawal. When they found it easy, they thought that was the end of the matter. But they hadn't looked at all the issues and beliefs like you are doing now, so sure enough, they started smoking again and were confused and bemused.

What if you want to go away for a few days, perhaps with a friend to support you? Fine, but does that mean you can't live smoke free today? Because if that's what it means then that thought is keeping you smoking today. If you are going away today, then fine do whatever you need to do but do it now because in addiction, tomorrow really never comes. How can there be a better time? The only time there is, is right now this minute. The past is dead and gone and the future is just a thought projection. The only reality is now. The truth will set you free and the truth is there is only now. There is not going to be a better time in the future. If you do come across that wonderful time in the future when it is ideal to stop smoking because there are no current issues or stresses or rough patches to get through, are you really going to spoil that lovely time by trying to stop smoking?

You may think that you understand all this and you know that the only time is now. Except that right now that reasonable voice is saying that 'now' is some time in the future when you have finished reading this book. This may never happen. So am I saying that you shouldn't wait until you have got to the end? No. I am saying wait this time because you are working on your addiction as you are reading this and you won't concentrate properly if you are having panic attacks. Since I am saying that there will be a better time then surely, there are better times than others? No. I am being very specific about this unique situation. Work through this course in a shorter time as possible and have your last cigarette when that time comes at the end of the course. I am not the voice of addiction.

I strongly suggest that you recognise that the voice of addiction is any thought that suggests it is ok to smoke now. This voice is part of you. Judging or hating it is the same as judging or hating yourself. Talk to this voice because it needs your guidance and love and reassurance that everything will be alright without that cigarette. It is a child and it wants you to be its parent. Talk to it like you talk to a child. Recognise that although it sounds like a grown-up it is still only a child and you can choose to reassure rather than scold or conquer.

I can't give up

In this section we will work through the thoughts associated with the belief you may have that you are unable to stop smoking. We will work through the various aspects of this belief, including the health and medical repercussions of being a smoker and the related consequences of stopping smoking. By the end of the section you will be free from this negative belief so that you are enabled to choose and you will have agreed to move forward with any medical consequences that may arise in the future.

The thought may well have crossed you mind that you can't give up. You have also probably thought that it is unlikely you will give up, or it would be a miracle if you gave up, or you just can't imagine giving up. The thought may also have crossed your mind that it's nearly impossible to give up, that it's very difficult to give up or it's too hard or really hard to give up.

Are any of these thoughts helpful at all? Is giving up smoking going to be easier with any of these thoughts floating around in your mind? We have two issues to work through. The first is obvious, the second is very subtle. The first issue is, what if any of these thoughts are actually true? What if we really will never be able to give up? It is a fear that is very real. Somewhere at the back of our minds is that millions of people have died from smoking because they were never able to stop. But, on the other hand, millions of people have stopped smoking. The first thought, that millions died because they did not give up, is completely true and has no doubt attached to it whatsoever. The second thought, that millions have given up, has doubts and is therefore weaker. The doubts include, *yes but many of those who stop start again; even though they have stopped it is too late because they still die from a smoking related disease;* and, *just because loads have stopped, who's to say I'm going to be one of them.*

Let's deal with each thought in turn.

1. *Many of those who stop start again.*

I have a friend who stopped smoking for two years, then he started again. Then he stopped again and he is still stopped. He might start again. That's the problem with stopping smoking, you might start again. That's why we are being released for life.

2. *People who have smoked in the past can still die from a smoking related disease.*

Well I know a bloke who smoked sixty a day for forty years and never had a day's illness in his life and eventually died from being run over by a bus. There are disturbing reports that passive smoking is a significant killer. Quite frankly, you are going to die, and it could be smoking related whether you smoke or not. If the reason you want to quit is because you are frightened of a smoking related death then I'm sorry, but I can't help you and you already knew that before you picked up this book. No, the real thought behind this thought is that they have been betrayed because they gave up a pleasure or crutch and made all that effort only to be punished anyway and that's worse than never having given up at all. Sods Law says that's bound to happen anyway. The problem is not death and illness themselves. The problem is the betrayal when you have made the effort to stop. It's God's/life's fault. You became a good person who didn't smoke anymore and God/Life punished you anyway by making you die from emphysema. At the end of this section there is an agreement. It is an official and binding contract that I want you think about very carefully before signing. It says that you agree to accept that if in the future you have a smoking related disease you will not blame anyone, including God/Life, yourself or others. It also says that you will not seek to punish yourself or anyone else by smoking, nor express your anger by smoking. You have to make a decision. The fact is you have smoked thousands of cigarettes over a long period of time and the damage may already have been done or it may manifest itself quite a long time after you have given up.

Here are a few statistics. I am not suggesting you believe these statistics as such because statistics are incredibly unreliable and generally misinterpreted anyway. There are lies, damn lies, and then there's statistics.

1.	2 to 12 Weeks	Circulation Improves.
2.	3 to 9 Months	Lung function increases by 10%.
3.	1 Year	Risk of heart attack falls to half that of a smoker.
4.	10 Years	Risk of lung cancer falls to half that of a smoker.
5.	15 Years	Risk of heart attack falls to same as someone who has never smoked.

These statistics can be viewed in a positive way, or in a negative way. According to a positive interpretation, we will be much fitter and healthier as a result of being smoke free. This is absolutely true, no problem with that whatsoever. The negative interpretation is that since it takes so long for the risk to fall to that of someone who has never smoked then what's the point in doing without a pleasure when it might well be too late anyway. As far as lung cancer is concerned the risk never falls to that of someone who has never smoked. I have heard that it's people who stop and start that run the most likelihood of getting cancer, so why rock the boat, why risk it?

It is obvious that the best way to view these statistics is the positive way. But we don't smoke for positive reasons, we smoke for negative reasons, so it is the negative reasons that need to be addressed. To continue smoking because we might die from a smoking related disease anyway is obviously very stupid indeed but simply putting a derogatory label like 'stupid' on to it is not very helpful. We need to make a decision that is final. The thought that we might be betrayed and die as a result of smoking anyway is a thought that will keep us smoking. Let's consider the possibilities. It isn't just about dying from lung cancer or heart attack, its living with the endless coughing and no sleep while you are waiting to die from lung cancer; it is living after the heart attack and having to change your diet and eat fruit and exercise regularly; it is living with amputated limbs and going through the operations and having to be dependent on others. The question you need to answer, is are you willing to face that if that is what is coming your way even if you stop smoking? That's where the contract comes in. You make a decision to agree to whatever is coming your way. We are all going to die. Because of smoking, some of us are going to die partially or wholly because we have smoked, regardless of giving up. Is it fair? No. Is it just? No. Is it right? No. But it is very likely to happen to some of us. Decide now, is it ok for what's coming to come anyway, or are you going to continue smoking because these awful things could certainly happen. Think about this very carefully, then sign the contract.

Please note: this is a contract between you and your sub-conscious self. It has got nothing to do with anyone else and could never be legally binding in any court of law.

Agreement

Agreement of Waiver of Medical Liability.

I, ... hereby declare to waive all medical liabilities which may arise in the future with respect to smoking related illnesses or possible smoking related illnesses, with respect to God and life and the universe and the force and spirit and soul and all other persons including tobacco merchants and manufacturers, advertising companies and all such people, places and things contributing to the shared illusions, mis-information and cover-ups with respect to nicotine addiction.

I also declare to waive all medical liabilities which may arise in the future with respect to smoking related illnesses or possible smoking related illnesses, with respect to myself including my past younger self and my recent past self and my present self, recognising addiction as a shared illusion thereby being only partially responsible for such medical conditions arising from past behaviour with regard to smoking addiction.

Signed and dated:

Signature: ....

Date: ....

Let's sum up the problems:-

If you stop you might start again
Making the effort to stop might be a waste of time
You might be one that never stops anyway

All these thoughts and problems are real. They are part of the reason people continue to smoke despite horrific illness, disease, death and financial problems. There is only one realistic answer. Don't try to stop smoking. It is futile. Don't make all that effort, missing out on the pleasure and help smoking offers you. You see, many people do stop smoking and they suffer and strive for years. We don't want to do that. We want to be free from this addiction. Being free means what it says - freedom. There is no struggle or being deprived or missing out or effort. We haven't "given up" anything; we are not missing out on anything. We no more struggle to "not smoke" than we struggle to "not eat sprouts". But wait a minute. We have never really enjoyed sprouts. But wait another minute, we don't and have never really enjoyed smoking. We have been in the grip of an addiction. We have been in a fog of illusion. We are now choosing to be free, and it's easy because we no longer suffer from the illusions that have kept us trapped and we have become totally aware of the nature of the addiction so it cannot trap us ever again. We certainly haven't stopped, or given up. We are not making an effort, or struggling, or missing out or looking back with fondness and affection. We are not lamenting the passing of our sick, insane slavery. That's the difference between we who are free and those who have given up.

OK, so the question now becomes, "can I be free?" The fact is, anyone, including yourself can be free. All those thoughts of whether you can give up or not no longer have any meaning. No-one is giving up anything. All those thoughts about needing a miracle are nonsense because there is no miracle in simply understanding the nature of the addiction and seeing the illusions for what they are. You no longer need to imagine giving up. You don't have to imagine anything. When you are free it is not hard or difficult not to smoke. Only people who have given up something and are thereby missing out on something are being deprived and are suffering now and again. People who are free have no such thoughts or illusions of pleasure or need. People who are free do not pine or crave or lament or suffer.

The thought that you can't give up is its own trap. It is a thought that stops you from being free. While ever you can't give up you are acknowledging there is something to give up, something of value, some pleasure or crutch that has use. Being free is about seeing those illusions. Being free means knowing there is no pleasure really, just an illusion of pleasure. Being free means knowing there is no crutch value in smoking, just illusions that smoking relieves uncomfortable feelings. When you have no single reason left to smoke, no illusions of pleasure or crutch, you simply don't smoke just as simply as you don't chew sandpaper.

I don't really want to stop smoking

In this section we will look at this major excuse that keeps smokers trapped in the addiction. We will also work through some fears about the future in relation to not smoking any more. We will look at other related beliefs regarding the pleasure associated with smoking and the mistaken belief that it takes strength and willpower to give up. By the end of the section you will be doubt free so that the question cannot arise again for you, and you will understand how love and understanding can set you free from this addiction.

I don't really want to stop smoking

Let's examine that. Is it?

That's why I haven't given up.
I enjoy it.
It's one of the few pleasures in life.
I can't face that massive gap there will be.
I still need to rebel.

"I don't want to give up really" provides a feasible explanation as to why you haven't given up yet. It also provides a reason by way of the pleasure and enjoyment. If I enjoy it so much then maybe I really don't want to give up? Behind that thought is the lie that smoking is a pleasure. We have already looked at this lie and we will be dealing with it in more detail later.

The idea that *"I don't want to give up really"* is a lie that every addict tells themselves each time the debate arises because it is disturbing and the lie stops the debate. Every time the question pops up about why you are risking death, disease and financial problems for an addiction that does absolutely nothing for you, the easiest way to get rid of the debate is to stand on your right to choose to smoke because you jolly well want to! Let us now test this theory, let us indulge in this debate for a moment, let's go there and not run away this time. Do you really want your daughter or son to smoke? Maybe you don't have children, but what if you did, would you want them to smoke is that what you would really want for them? No? So how come you want that for you? Do you want your nieces and nephews to smoke? What about your Father, Mother, Brother? What about anyone you care anything about at all - would you wish them to start smoking? What about the loved ones in your life who already smoke, wouldn't you prefer them to give up?

If you wish your loved ones to be non-smokers then why do you say you choose to smoke? It can't be that great if you don't want your loved ones to do it. It is often easier to love others than it is to love ourselves so let me put the question another way. Do the people who love you (not you, obviously) want you to continue smoking or not? I think enough has been said. In truth, just about every smoker wants to give up really and it is only the shame of continuing that compels this lie to one's self that you don't really want to stop.

Saying I don't want to give up really can also be a form of self pity – i.e. my life is so bad it is one of the few pleasures I have. This particular point needs further explanation. It is very easy for a non-smoking, smug smartperson like myself to pour scorn on a bit of self pity about smoking being one of the few pleasures you have in your life, but it is actually a very serious point. If you believe smoking is a pleasure and if you indulge in your pleasure 20, 40 or 60 times a day every singe day of your life, then there isn't going to be much room left in your life to explore, develop and enjoy other forms of pleasure. So the truth becomes – smoking is one of the few pleasures in your life because there isn't time to explore new pleasures or new pleasures that involve doing without smoking for any length of time. The other subtle aspect of this thought that smoking is your only or one of the few pleasures in your life is that it creates a feeling of shame and low self-esteem. The more shame you feel in your heart, the more comfort you feel you need, the greater is your dependence on anything resembling comfort such as smoking. The more shame you feel about yourself the more fear you have of what others think. The more fear you have, the more you feel you need comfort the more you seem to need to smoke. So altogether the thought that smoking is one of your few pleasures supports your need to smoke in lots of ways. So how do we deal with this particular thought so that we don't feel so shameful and fearful and in need of comfort?

We do it by knowing that smoking is not a real pleasure. The only pleasure involved is the release from the discomfort created by the last cigarette. But you might say that although I understand that, it is still true that pleasure is felt. Yes of course it is, but surely if you wanted such an insane hobby as experiencing the pleasure felt from previously self inflicted pain, carry a rubber band around with you all the time or try a few trips to Miss Whiplash or Mr Spankhard who will delight you with even more extreme pain and pleasurable relief. If, at the end of the day you insist you cannot give up this false pleasure then continue smoking and be happy. On the other hand, you could choose to recognise that the real issue here is not that you are missing that very dubious pleasure but that it is too much of a loss to tolerate. So let's look at the consequences of this loss.

You will lose feeling uncomfortable and peculiar and sometimes panicky every half-hour and you will lose the feeling of relief from these uncomfortable feelings each time that you smoke. You can only miss this pleasure of relief if you have the withdrawal feelings in the first place. A non-smoker cannot have that pleasure or relief by having a cigarette because there are no withdrawals there from which to be relieved. The cigarette cannot work. As a non-smoker you cannot miss the pleasure of relief because you know that a cigarette will do nothing for you. If you have ever gone for a time without smoking you will know that the first cigarette did nothing for you except perhaps make you feel dizzy or a little sick and it also tasted foul. The next cigarette after the first one will give you relief from the withdrawals of the first one. All of which has nothing to do with solving your feelings of discomfort that triggered the thought of smoking in the first place. Smoking will not solve your problem or genuinely make you feel better.

The next issue is the gap in your life that is created by the absence of smoking. There are actually several gaps here. The physical gap of cigarettes not being there and the gap of time you have where you are not smoking any more. There is also a gap inside that is a feeling of emptiness or spiritual void. This gap is dealt with elsewhere.

The physical gap. Where there used to be a cigarette there is no longer a cigarette. For example: there are your pockets. No longer will you need to check your pockets to make sure you have your cigarettes or your lighter. When you find yourself checking after you have become free it is a wonderful thing because it is an opportunity to be happy that you are free and you might find you don't even need to put on that coat or jacket because you don't have to carry your cigarettes and lighter around everywhere you go anymore. It's a wonderful experience because you see just how much like a ball and chain it is to have to carry those cigarettes with you every single place you go. Unfortunately, this business of checking doesn't last very long at all, but for however long it does last it just gives you opportunities to feel fantastic about being free. So where else are there cigarettes now where there won't be when you are free? Why in the ashtrays of course. Unfortunately you probably will not experience missing the ashtrays at all, but if you do that is another opportunity to be glad about your freedom. Where else could you miss cigarettes? In your hand, between your fingers, and in your mouth. It has been said that sucking on a cigarette provides comfort because it is like a baby sucking on mother's teat or using a dummy. Some people have been known to suck on dummy cigarettes so they don't miss their sucking comfort (you have to be careful how you say that). When we were babies we had this awful empty feeling that made us panic but we learned that sucking on a breast or bottle filled that empty feeling. We later found out that we were hungry, but the sucking and filling came with cuddles and love and acceptance and a feeling of being precious and valuable so even the act of sucking seemed to fill and comfort us. However, the fact is, we grew out of that and by the time we started smoking, sucking on dummies and thumbs no longer worked for us. We did not become addicted to smoking because we were trying to replace the missing breast or dummy and that is why sucking on another object instead of smoking cannot work. Non smokers do not suck on anything for comfort instead of smoking. Ex smokers do not miss the sucking because smoking is not really sucking is it? It's more like just breathing in because you're not actually swallowing anything and there is no bodily contact with anyone else to give you feelings of love and acceptance etc. I hope you can now see that ex-smokers who are free do not miss the sucking – not at all.

What about the missing cigarette between the fingers? Before we deal with the missing aspect, let's get this thing into perspective. If you smoke forty a day and it takes five minutes to smoke each cigarette, that's a total of two hundred minutes, that is, three and a half hours each day. So for three and a half hours each day you are holding a cigarette between your fingers. What on earth are going to do with your hands for that three and a half hours every day? Well, since you are awake for sixteen hours a day, what do you do with your hands the other twelve and a half hours anyway? Well whatever nasty little habits you get up to with those little fingers, maybe you could just do them some more. It is a myth that you don't know what to do with your hands when you give up smoking. How has this myth come into being? People have been known to say that when they give up smoking they don't know what to do with their hands. This of course is absolute nonsense so why do they say that? When people stop smoking without the benefit of the knowledge in these pages, they become anxious and nervous and therefore fidgety. When you are fidgety you want to do something with your hands and fingers. If you are aware you are fidgety because you are giving up smoking then it is natural for you to assume that it is the absence of the cigarettes in your fingers that is causing the fidgetiness. The fact that for twelve and a half hours every day of your smoking life previously you didn't experience that fidgetiness when you weren't smoking is easily forgotten. But the fact is, it is not the absence of a cigarette in your fingers that you are missing. Even putting a cigarette in your fingers will not stop the fidgetiness.

Now that you are aware, you are now free from all that nonsense and you will no longer feel that you don't know what to do with your hands, it just doesn't happen. You will not miss the cigarettes in your fingers, hands, mouths and pockets. If anything it is just a wonderful feeling that you can enjoy for a short while that you are free and you have much more freedom of movement in all sorts of ways.

It takes strength and will power to give up

Let's take a look at this. How much strength and willpower does it take to give up? It doesn't actually take any strength or will power to not smoke. It may seem to take great determination and effort to not smoke but in reality it takes none whatsoever. It is the focus that creates this illusion, a focus on something outside yourself. To fight the addiction you need something to blame for it so that you can have something fight. People blame the cigarettes, or the nicotine. Or they may be aware that it is not the cigarettes or the nicotine that is to blame, but the addiction. This doesn't work because if you blame the addiction, or the drug nicotine, the focus is still on the outside.

The truth is that the addiction is within us. The addiction is a complex interplay of illusions between the conscious and the sub-conscious mind that triggers feelings. The addiction therefore is our thoughts. Our thoughts are part of us. So of course, when you try and fight the cigarettes or the nicotine it is a complete waste of time because it is not they that are responsible. Every attempt to fight this addiction can only ever be a fight with ourselves. When you fight this addiction you are fighting yourself. That is why it seems to take great strength and willpower. You are fighting an equal force when you fight with yourself. In fact, it could be said that the more strength and willpower you have, the more strength and willpower you will need with which to fight yourself. People who display tremendous strength and willpower in other areas of their lives still can be defeated fighting this addiction.

The more you regard this business as a fight the less likely you are to win it, simply because it is yourself you are fighting. May I suggest a path that works? Love and understanding. Understand that addiction is a set of illusions that simply need exposing and bringing into the light of reality. Love yourself by understanding that you were given these illusions and this is not your fault. Love yourself enough to stop calling yourself names like 'stupid' or 'weak' or 'pathetic' just because you are the victim of illusions you did not make up yourself. Love yourself enough to recognise that millions of other people are also victims of these illusions and that doesn't make you any less. Understand that there is nothing to fight, only the truth to see. You love yourself enough to read, and do the exercises in, this course so you love yourself enough to live addiction free. You already have enough love for yourself. You have understood that you need help to become free and you will come to understand so much more by working through this course that you will be free.

There is another aspect to this lie that we need to look at. It is not strength and willpower we need to become free from this addiction. It is strength and willpower we need to continue smoking day in, day out for the whole of our lives. It takes great strength and willpower to get to the all night garage in the middle of winter to spend money we can ill afford to buy something that creates filth, death, disease and financial hardship. It takes incredible strength and willpower to stop smoking without becoming free and spending the rest of our lives missing out on that pleasure and foregoing the tremendous help cigarettes used to give us to cope with life. That takes strength, willpower and guts but most of all complete and utter insanity. The kind of insanity that shines through the tremendous strength and willpower it takes to commit such a slow kind of pointless suicide.

Cutting down works

In this section we will look at whether cutting down works, what is genuine withdrawal and what about cigars and pipes. By the end of this section you will no longer have any doubts about the insanity of an addict entertaining half measures and you will have permanent freedom from this common debate.

There is an idea that cutting down works. You may dismiss this idea out of hand, but nevertheless there may be a part of you that entertains the possibility. There are two aspects to this idea.

a)   Cut down to a level of smoking that is acceptable in terms of health and finance.

b)   Cutting down gradually so that it is easier to stop completely

Regarding point a. This is a smoking cessation course not a 'let's carry on being a deluded addict by making it acceptable' course. There are smokers who claim they enjoy the occasional smoke. I am not one of them, it is something I do not know how to do, but I will deal with this issue later because we are here to deal with all issues.

Firstly though, we will look at the idea of cutting down gradually in order to stop completely at some stage in the future. This is a very logical idea that seems to deal with the physical aspects of withdrawal and the fear of living smoke free. The physical aspect of the idea goes like this - a gradual withdrawal of the chemical from the body means that the body and mind get used to a lower level of the substance so that when you stop completely there is little or no physical discomfort, or at least such a low level of discomfort that it makes giving up possible. This is actually how nicotine patches are supposed to work. However, there is a slight flaw in the logical, simple, brilliant plan - it's complete and utter nonsense! The physical withdrawal from nicotine happens between ten and twenty minutes after the last cigarette and the physical symptoms are so slight they don't even wake us up from our sleep, they don't even stop us going to sleep. Ok, let's say Graham is wrong and this cutting down gradually idea is really true and really does work. Let's go through what is happening here again because it is important to be very clear and doubt free about this in order to be free.

Now please say out loud six times – just do it!

> **These** feelings and this confusion will pass whether I smoke or not.
> These feelings and this confusion **will** pass whether I smoke or not.
> These feelings and this confusion will **pass** whether I smoke or not.
> These feelings and this confusion will pass **whether** I smoke or not.
> These feelings and this confusion will pass whether **I** smoke or not.
> These feelings and this confusion will pass whether I smoke **or not**.

Either there is genuine physical withdrawal or there isn't

Let's just say, for argument's sake, there is actual physical withdrawal. OK, how bad is it? Is it more or less than food poisoning? Is it more or less than the flue or a bad cold? Is it worse than or easier than a mild case of diarrhoea? How long does it last? Three months? Three weeks? Two weeks? Ten days, five days, three days, two days? If it lasts three weeks, does it get gradually easier or worse until it suddenly stops? Does it gradually get worse for a time until it begins to gradually get better? Does this vary from individual to individual because our bodies are genetically different? Is my body more genetically in need of nicotine than so and so's? What are the symptoms of withdrawal? Higher blood pressure, faster breathing, tight throat - ooh, no sorry, they are the symptoms of actually smoking aren't they, that tremendous physical pleasure we get from the reaction our bodies have to the enforced inhalation of toxic fumes. Sorry, those things are good things apparently, they are the reason we smoke. So what are the symptoms of withdrawal? Tight bladder, slight queasiness in the stomach, feeling uncomfortable like you need to move because you can't stay still, sweating, heavier breathing. Just a minute, they are the exact same symptoms you get when you are anxious or are having a panic attack. Those symptoms are the result of adrenaline produced by psychological fear so that you can fight or flight. Is it a coincidence that nicotine withdrawal symptoms are exactly the same as the symptoms of an increased adrenaline level brought on by anxiety or fear? If we are genetically different, how come we all feel these feelings the moment we decide never to smoke again?

OK, let's get real. The truth is there aren't any physical withdrawals from nicotine. There is just an increased adrenaline level. We have a panic attack because there is anxiety; something has left our brain rather quickly and it produces a sense of loss and threat that our sub-conscious mind hasn't up until now been able to understand. We don't get these symptoms when we go to bed, or when we are on the plane, because we know we will be able to smoke later, so that little sense of loss of something missing is very easy to cope with in a conscious way. No anxiety or fear, no symptoms. There are no physical symptoms from nicotine withdrawal, there is only fear and fear has physical symptoms.

As soon as a nicotine addict makes a decision to quit the decision creates some understandable anxiety and fear. Whenever a person is anxious or fearful, the sub-conscious mind senses a threat and stimulates the adrenal gland to produce a tiny amount of adrenaline just in case we have to fight or take flight. The adrenaline then has a physical effect on our bodies, increasing the heart rate, causing quicker breathing and raising our body temperature etc. We feel this as a slight flushed feeling like what we have when we have been caught doing something naughty or embarrassing. These physical sensations cause us some added concern on top of the existing anxiety as we seek to find some meaning to them. The addiction illusions are then used by our conscious minds, and the fears about going nuts, failures, missing out etc come up and this causes us more anxiety and fear. The sub-conscious mind detects our increase in anxiety and fear and does the job it is supposed to do, stimulating the adrenal gland to give us a bit more adrenaline because it looks like the threat is greater than was first thought. The ensuing physical feelings from this dose of adrenaline reinforce our addiction beliefs and fears and the level of fear and anxiety rises once again. In response to this there is more adrenaline produced and then more physical symptoms and then more fear and panic.

This goes on and on and on until there is complete and utter panic.

PANIC
PANIC
PANIC

We then light a cigarette and once again the lies that cigarettes help us relax and we would go nuts without them is reinforced in our minds as being the truth.

If you didn't know this; you would mistake the adrenaline reaction as a physical withdrawal from nicotine. That being the case, you would see another smoke as being the solution to that discomfort. Eventually you could go on to mistakenly believe that smoking is actually a pleasure. In which case, should you ever stop smoking; you would feel you were missing out on a pleasure, every single day for the rest of your life. That is no way to live and it is only a matter of time and painful events before you are smoking again. Two choices, a life of being deprived or a life of struggle. You don't need either, because it is all nonsense in the first place.

Let's say there is no way you would mistake smoking as being an actual pleasure. Let's say you are already well beyond believing that particular piece of nonsense. Nevertheless, if you believe that there are withdrawals caused by the nicotine, then it still seems a good idea to do a gradual withdrawal or use patches for the same reason. But there is a problem with this. You could resist smoking and cut down on the physical withdrawals, but you would not be free. Being free is a state of mind, not a physical situation. Being free is living in the truth, not dodging a mistaken belief on a day to day basis. If there is any belief in withdrawal, it must follow that there could be relief from withdrawal in the form of nicotine, either smoking, chewing or patches. That being the case, for the rest of your life, in your mind, nicotine has the potential for relief of discomfort. Even if you don't believe in the pleasure of nicotine, you can still have a belief in the relief value of nicotine. Because in reality there really is no such thing as physical withdrawal from nicotine, your mind can only identify discomfort from natural physical reactions to everyday feelings such as anxiety, fear, panic, tiredness. So your mind is forced to believe it is missing out on a source of relief from these perfectly natural uncomfortable physical reactions to everyday feelings. This is a con, a mistake, a case of being stark, staringly wrong. You see, if there really was genuine, identifiable physical symptoms from nicotine withdrawal, once you had got through them, you would never feel those feelings again. The fact that these symptoms don't exist, means that you mistakenly identify real physical sensations about other things as something that nicotine can help relieve.

If you have ever stopped smoking for a while before, you will remember that the first cigarette created uncomfortable physical reactions, it made you cough, feel sick, tasted nasty, it did not relive the uncomfortable feelings you had before. The inhalation of toxic fumes may have diverted your attention away from the original problem that created the uncomfortable feelings in the first place and robbed you of the opportunity to grow through the problem by creating an even bigger problem - you have started smoking again and the next cigarette will relieve the withdrawal from that first one. You are back in the pit; you are once again a slave. It's the first one that does it. But that first cigarette did not relieve any of the uncomfortable feelings you had originally. The fact that you started smoking again added feelings of remorse, guilt, disappointment, low self-esteem and anger; you now have all those emotions to cope with and you still believe nicotine will help you. You now need to smoke even more and the whole sick, insane, sorry carry-on starts up all over again, yet again. But the second cigarette does relieve the withdrawal created by the first so that's alright then isn't it?

Just returning to the land of the sane for a moment, does cutting down work at all? After all, nicotine patches have reportedly helped some people. The main difficulty in becoming free is fear. The part of you that is the addict is like a child that cannot trust everything will be OK. If you are faced with a period of time when you cannot smoke, but you know you will be able to smoke within a certain time frame, fear and panic are kept at bay. This period of time, smoke free, without too much fear and panic helps that part of you to accept that there isn't much to really fear in the land of smoke-freeness. The fact that you know you will smoke again in four hours, or tomorrow, helps that child part of you accept that there won't be a cigarette to suck on for a while, but it's OK.

Let's just talk about patches for a while, because cutting down smoking and cutting down with patches are two different things. Patches claim to reduce withdrawal by supplying the drug in a different way for a while so you don't suffer withdrawals even though you don't smoke. What they actually do is con that child part of you that is the addict that it's safe to not smoke because there won't be much suffering so there won't be any need to smoke. If you can believe this story then patches can help you stop smoking. If this has not worked for you, or you really cannot buy into this story, then there is no real point in trying patches again. Ultimately they work by telling a lie to cover up a lie. They lie that they relieve the physical withdrawals that don't really exist anyway. It's all about what you believe. Patches support a belief - that nicotine chemically relieves some form of stress. That can come back on you later. You are not really free; you simply have a reprieve, and you don't know how long it will last. The only real solution is to be honest and see the truth. Withdrawal is not physical, it is psychological. There are many people who have seen through the illusions and have become genuinely free after they stopped smoking by using patches, but also there are many that have used patches who are not free. Being free from this addiction is knowing without doubt that the only suffering is because of a mistaken belief that nicotine does something it doesn't and cannot do. Without that belief there can be no dependence or desire or need to smoke.

Cigars and pipes are ok

There are some people who stopped smoking by smoking cigars and pipes instead of cigarettes. So what's the difference? Well, they say, you don't have to inhale pipes and cigars so there is not the same danger to health and you don't get addicted.

These two points need discussing. First of all, the fact that not inhaling is less risky to your health may or may not be true but this is irrelevant because it has nothing do to with anything. It is a crazy and stupid statement that does not address the issue but simply leads you away from the issue. So what if you don't inhale? If you didn't inhale cigarettes they may well be less hazardous to health too.

The other point that is sometimes made is that it is not addictive if you don't inhale. The problem with this lie is that if it isn't addictive, how can you experience the pleasure of relief from the withdrawal? Why is it that putting nicotine in your bloodstream through only your tongue and gums instead of through your lungs suddenly makes the nicotine less addictive? Because less nicotine gets through? Are you sure? So less nicotine is less addictive is it? Of course not! To a nicotine addict less nicotine is more addictive. If I'm right about this and they are wrong then why are they less addicted to their pipes and cigars than a cigarette smoker is addicted to cigarettes? The answer is very simple. Nicotine addiction is so weak they don't even notice it. Since they don't suffer from genuine addiction, i.e. the illusions, they only notice the actual physical withdrawal enough to enjoy the foul smoke that gives them that slight relief, much the same as a tea or coffee drinker enjoys their drink. Caffeine is also slightly addictive; that is why you can drink that amount of tea or coffee throughout the day and not get sick of it. You try drinking a non addictive drink that much through the day: it would make you feel sick. Because tea and coffee have an addictive drug in them people can drink gallons of the stuff and not get sick of it just the same as a pipe or cigar smoker or a cigarette smoker or a coke sniffer or a heroin shooter. To an addict a thousand is never enough and one is too many.

The difference lies in the beliefs about the addiction. You expect to go nuts if you stop smoking; you don't expect to go nuts if you don't light your pipe or smoke your cigar. You don't expect to go nuts if you don't drink your tea. But try to stop drinking tea and coffee and you could well find it is quite difficult. In fact you might be surprised how much you would miss it. You may even feel that if you don't get a drink soon you will go nuts. Of course different drugs have different addictive effect. Heroin has a much more addictive effect than caffeine and nicotine. The addictive strength of the drug nicotine is very similar to that of caffeine. There are two proofs of this I want to show you now. One, you can be a pipe or cigar smoker and not feel such a strong addiction as a cigarette smoker to the same drug because of different expectations, not because the drug is any different. This proves that the actual physical addiction is very weak. The other proof is in relation to heroin addiction. No-one, I'm sure, would disagree that the drug heroin is far, far more addictive than nicotine. Despite this, you will find that just about all ex heroin addicts will tell you it is far more difficult to stop smoking than it is to come off heroin. How can this be if the drug itself is so weak? Because addiction as a set of beliefs is more powerful than any drug could ever hope to be. You can't get past this point. There are extremely few, if any, ex heroin addicts who will tell you it was easy to come off heroin. There are loads of ex-smokers who will tell you that it was a lot easier than they thought it would be. There are many pipe smokers and cigar smokers who are not addicted because the withdrawal from the nicotine they have put into their system is so weak they can very easily be ignorant that it was ever there. Same drug.

Some more truth. Many of these pipe smokers and cigar smokers to which you refer simply do not exist except in the minds of struggling addicts. In reality very, very few people who smoke a pipe would give it up so easily. They have no need to do that because they are not addicted so they don't have to give up. It is also true to say the vast majority of people who smoked cigarettes and then went on to smoke pipes or cigars instead eventually ended up back on cigarettes or both. It is also true that most people who smoke cigars do so for image and macho reasons because you know they do actually taste foul. If you are a nicotine addict whether on a cigar or pipe you will eventually inhale, you have no choice. One is too many and a thousand never enough.

Part 3

Illusions

All I need is a short time not smoking

In this section we will look at the beliefs/illusions about the length of time an ex-smoker suffers from withdrawal symptoms. Using this example illusion you will be shown a process of how to deal with feelings and thoughts associated with withdrawals. By the end of the section you will have learned a process by which you can deal with any withdrawal feelings that arise so that you become free from them all for the rest of your life.

The logic goes like this –

I hate smoking so much; if I just had a certain amount of time, just to get over the withdrawals, just to get over that hump, then I would never go back to smoking. I can't understand people who have had 3 weeks, 3 months, 6 months, a year, 2 years not smoking, then suddenly start again. They got free from this awful addiction and then they started again. It must be that just one cigarette does it. So why have the one?

All such thoughts might seem like good thoughts to have. Like putting money in the bank so that when you stop you won't be one of those people who start again. Except that most of us had these thoughts when we first started smoking – it won't happen to me, I'll stop before any damage is done blah di blah di blah. There is some truth about the thought that, *"once I am over the hump, I will be ok"*, but it depends on your perception of the hump. The most common perception of this hump is a period of withdrawal, sweating, feeling uncomfortable, not eating, eating too much and generally being obsessed about not smoking. Since the physical sensations are due to our thoughts then getting over that hump is when we stop thinking about the issue and think about other things instead. And furthermore, here I am thinking about this issue and I'm not in any distress at all, so in the end, getting over the hump is working through the particular thoughts that cause the panic attacks. Not all thoughts about smoking induce a physical reaction. **Getting over the hump means working through all the thoughts that cause any kind of physical reaction.**

Working through the thoughts means:-

1. Detaching from the feeling.
2. Facing the thought squarely.
3. Holding it up to the light to see the illusion and that particular thought's connections to other thoughts and issues.
3. Coming to a settlement, a peace about it so that there is no longer any point in thinking about it.

(Trigger Event)

Detach from feeling –
identify symptoms

Identify the Thought –
(and related thoughts)

Identify the Illusion –
See there is no need/pleasure

Acceptance/Freedom

You have faced it, so there is no longer any fear, therefore there is no physical reaction. Which thoughts cause all the physical and emotional distress and which thoughts don't? Well, that's a personal thing. Some smokers have a strong physical reaction to, *I need a cig because I need to concentrate* and some don't. Other smokers have a strong physical reaction to, *I am missing out on such a familiar pleasure after sex* and others don't. Of course, many thoughts that create physical distress and discomfort are shared by all or most smokers. The majority of thoughts that cause withdrawal feelings are common to most and those are the thoughts that we are dealing with in this course. But brains are complicated. They may look like lumps of jelly, but you get a microscope and look at all that internal wiring and the complexity is mind boggling. People smoke again because a thought that had not been worked through comes up and causes a panic attack. It was tucked away in the sub-conscious, in all the complex wiring. It was never addressed in the first place, it was run away from, it was not faced.

Does this mean that in a couple of years there might be a thought that comes upon you that causes a panic attack when you are in a vulnerable situation and you might smoke again? No. Because, it's not the thoughts themselves that cause the smoking, it's the fear of those thoughts that causes the smoking, it's how you are set up to deal with those thoughts that will determine control of fear and the situation.

Working through thoughts and feelings

If you know that the feeling is caused by a thought and you ask the question, *"Why? What's this about?"* and you go through the process of working through it, then you will not smoke. If you don't know what to do then you will want to run away and if you can't, then you will smoke. It is fear and ignorance that causes relapse. Fear of the feelings, ignorance and fear of the thoughts that are causing the feelings and ignorance of the working through process. It is the process of working through that is the key to freedom, not wishing things away and running away. When you know the process you are already free and you are free for ever regardless of any thoughts, feelings and issues that arise.

Let me give you an example. I was in a bus station the other day and there was someone smoking. I enjoyed the smell of the smoke yet there was no panic attack, or craving, or fear, or wishing or self pity because I was deprived. Why? Because I already know that it only smells pleasant to me because it's a familiar reaction and therefore comforting. That's why. I know the truth is that smoke doesn't really smell nice at all, it is just an illusion. I also know that I am not missing out on any pleasure at all. Since I am not withdrawing I can't experience the pleasure of relief from withdrawal, so my smoking a cigarette right now could not give me pleasure. It would make me dizzy and sick and drag me back into the pit. I am well practised in waiting for a bus without smoking, so there is no perception of need. To sum up, I knew there was an illusion. I knew why there was an illusion. I knew I was not missing out on a pleasure and I knew I had no need. Peace, acceptance. No panic, no self pity, no longing or craving or anything, just gratitude that I am free from all that head mess. Grateful that I have been given the truth and that the truth has set me and is keeping me free. Get that process under your belt. First, by learning how to do it by doing the exercises in this course, then by practising it whenever the opportunity presents itself no matter how long it takes.

Let's look at symptoms of withdrawal. Dizziness, hunger, depression, anger, sickness, fear, panic, aching muscles, wobbly legs, wobbly guts, tight bladders, loose bladders, etc. When you are experiencing symptoms, first of all recognise the physical feelings. Identify what you are experiencing on a physical level. This is good advice whether you are a smoker or not, this is not just about withdrawals, do it anyway. Get in touch with the physical aspect of whatever it is you are feeling. Not the issue behind it or the possible reason why, that is just justification or trying to understand. The very first thing to do every time is to connect with your body. The physical experience that your body is having. Identify it. How is my breathing? Is it short or deep or quick or slow? How is my stomach? Is it tight, is there sharp pain, is there nausea is there tightness in the pit. How is my throat. . . . By doing this, you are separating your physical sensations from your issues. You are stopping the process of piling symptoms on top of symptoms. You are not allowing these physical feeling to worry and frighten you so that you feel more physical feelings of anxiety and stress by focusing on the issues and fears. You are simply isolating and identifying physical sensations instead of getting involved in issues and head mess. Once you have a good grip of what you are feeling on a physical level you will then be detached and safe enough to go through the rest of the process of working through the identification of the thought that created the feeling, the illusion that supports this thought and reason why it is an illusion.

Here is an exercise for you to do. Answer the questions on the exercise on a separate piece of paper. Use the **list of situations/thoughts/feelings** to work through.

This exercise is designed to help you develop a way of dealing with the thoughts and feelings that arise as a result of addiction. By the end of the exercise you will be able to work through any thoughts or feelings that may have been a threat to you before you learned this process.

Select a few examples from the list of **situations/thoughts/feelings** *below that seem relevant to you. Imagine it is you in that situation having those thoughts and feelings. Write down in your own words the answers to the questions listed below. Remember, there are no wrong answers, it is the process which is important. Soon you will be* *able to do this with any thoughts and feelings that previously may have persuaded you to smoke.*

1.   *What is the situation?*

2.   *What are the thoughts around this situation?*

3.   *What would you call the feeling (fear, anger, anxiety, craving)?*

4.   *What are the physical symptoms of this feeling (higher heart rate, feeling flushed, sweaty, wobbly, butterflies in stomach)?*

5.   *What is the illusion that is feeding this thought, and why is it an illusion?*

6.   *What will happen if you choose to smoke?*

7.   *What will happen if you choose to remain smoke free?*

List of situations/thoughts/feelings.

Situation: *Fancying someone at a party and considering chatting them up, but they smoke.*

Thought: *Will he/she accept a non-smoker or will this cause problems in the relationship.*

Feeling: *Vulnerable, insecure – possible rejection.*

Situation: *Getting up first thing in the morning and having your tea or coffee.*

Thought: *I have always enjoyed a smoke first thing with my tea/coffee.*

Feeling: *Fear of suffering because of missing out.*

Situation: *Going to the toilet.*

Thought: *I won't be able to go without a cigarette.*

Feeling: *Fear of being constipated.*

Situation: *Finishing a meal and friends/colleagues lighting up.*

Thought: *Why can't I enjoy a cigarette like them.*

Feeling: *Fear that you might smoke.*

Situation: *Driving my car.*

Thought: *I always used to smoke while driving.*

Feeling: *Fear of the driving triggering withdrawal/panic feelings.*

Situation: *Going for a job interview.*

Thought: *Smoking would calm my nerves and help me cope.*

Feeling: *Insecurity without the crutch.*

Situation: *You are far away in a hotel in the bar.*
Thought: *Nobody will know if I have a smoke now.*
Feeling: *Fear of missing out on this opportunity.*

Situation: *Having to finish some work that requires concentration.*
Thought: *I can't concentrate without smoking.*
Feeling: *Fear of not finishing the work and getting sacked or not getting paid.*

Now think of two situations of your own and work through those.

Doing this exercise will take time and effort. Please take that time and make the effort, it is the key to your permanent freedom. Learning this process is what will set you free for life. Do not just read through it and come back to it later. Stop reading now and do this exercise. Get into detail with it. Look at all the possible connotations of thoughts and feelings you have in each and every situation. Take this seriously because the more thorough you are with this exercise, the deeper you go, the more detailed you are, the more courage you can find to do this, the better for you and the greater will be and the sooner will come your freedom. The more time you take doing this exercise the sooner will be your ultimate freedom from nicotine addiction. The exercise is complicated. Just take it one question at a time. There are no wrong answers, what matters is you making the effort to try to answer the questions.

Smoking is a pleasure?

In this section we will look at the belief that smoking is a pleasure. By the end of this section you will be free from the illusion that smoking could ever be a genuine pleasure.

Before we move on, let's address this belief. We will address this later as well, in terms of taste and the times when it seems more pleasurable than others. I once read a theory that said only certain cigarettes actually are pleasurable, like the ones after meals and sex and with alcohol etc. The truth is, no cigarettes are pleasurable, so certain cigarettes can't possibly be more pleasurable than others. Let's go back to the example I mentioned earlier that smoking is like pinching yourself, or giving yourself a pain in order to relieve the pain. That relief from pain is actually a pleasure to experience. When you're out in the cold and rain, the experience of relief when you get in and experience warmth and dryness is very pleasurable. If you have been hungry a while and you eat some bland, dry bread and water, that is pleasurable even though it doesn't taste great, because the relief from hunger is a pleasurable experience in itself, just like the relief from nicotine withdrawal is a pleasurable experience in itself. It is not the actual smoking that is the pleasure; it is the relief from the psychological withdrawal that seems like a pleasure. There are two things to think about here. It isn't sane to give yourself pain simply to experience the pleasure of the relief from that pain. Also, the only people who can get the so-called pleasure of relief from withdrawal are addicts who are withdrawing. A non-smoker, or a first time smoker or even an ex-smoker can't do that because they are not withdrawing.

If you have ever given up smoking for a short while you will know that that first cigarette is much like the first cigarette you ever smoked. There was no pleasure involved. The ones after gave the pleasure of relief from withdrawal, but that first one couldn't because you weren't withdrawing at the time, because you had not smoked in a while. So the pleasure of that relief can only be felt by people who have recently had a cigarette. If you haven't had one for a while, you have to get back into the whole addiction cycle again for that relief experience to work. One cigarette doesn't do it.

The fear is, *will I miss that pleasure?* This is a serious question and it must be answered completely, positively and without doubt. Do you go out into the wind and rain just to experience coming into the warmth and for no other reason? Have you ever starved yourself so that the food would be more of a pleasure to eat, to get more relief from hunger pains? Maybe you do choose to wear a tight belt or girdle if that takes your fancy for a while solely in order to experience the pleasure of the relief when you take it off. You may clamp your nipples with bulldog clips to experience the pleasure of the pain and the relief from pain, nothing wrong with that, we've all done it, I know I have, but sane people don't do that twenty or thirty or forty times a day, every single day for years and years.

Imagine doing an experiment. Imagine putting on a tight, uncomfortable belt or girdle and taking it off again twenty times a day for the next three months, so that you get into the habit of experiencing the pleasure of taking it off again twenty times a day. Do you think you would continue to do that after the three months? Of course not. So there must be more to it than that. You don't continue smoking and risking your life, spending all that money and living in this slavery just for the pleasure of the relief from withdrawals do you? Of course not. The idea that you will miss this pleasure is nonsense. We smoke for other reasons than that. If we smoked just for the pleasure of experiencing relief twenty times a day then we would stop doing that easily. We don't smoke for pleasure. We don't put up with the cost and the slavery for that pleasure. When we are free from our illusions we will no more want to experience that pleasure than we would want to go out and buy an uncomfortable tight belt or go out in the wind and rain for ten minutes. You cannot and will not miss it! You cannot and will not miss that pleasure of relief from the pain and fear of withdrawals, and since that is the only pleasure involved, you will simply choose not to do it in the same way you choose not to inflict any kind of pain or discomfort on yourself just in order to get pleasure from relieving it. The problem is that we are not convinced that relief from withdrawal is the only pleasure. We think it tastes nice, helps us relax, helps us concentrate etc blah di blah di blah ad nauseum. When you know different, you cannot miss such an insane and dubious pleasure.

We have already looked at how a thought creates a feeling, that is, behind every feeling is a thought, and we have seen that this is also why smoking is a pleasure. You have a thought or a small number of thoughts that trigger a pleasure response. As I mentioned in the previous paragraph, the mistaken thoughts of *"it tastes nice; it's relaxing"* etc are the usual sorts of illusions connected to the pleasure centre of the brain. So when you smoke you do experience pleasure. When you see through the illusions it is impossible for you to experience pleasure from smoking because quite simply, smoking is an obnoxious and disturbing thing to do. It is these illusions themselves that link smoking with the belief it is a pleasure. These illusions are taught to us when we are young and even non-smokers believe them.

The reason so many people have found smoking easy to give up is because they have seen through the illusions and as we know, the actual chemical addictiveness of smoking is very, very weak – like caffeine. The pleasures you think you feel are conditioned into your conscious mind. However because they are illusions, when we first try smoking we can only experience the reality, which is that it is disturbing and obnoxious. The trouble is, we are people and quite often disturbing and obnoxious things can appeal to us, particularly if they are dangerous. For example, roller coaster rides for some people can be wonderful and pleasurable. That is not the reality. It is in reality disturbing and frightening but we can turn it into the opposite. If you found a roller coaster ride pleasurable for some time and then suddenly focussed on the reality of the danger and the actual physical effects then you might no longer enjoy or find pleasure in it. You would probably give it up and you would not miss it. You would not crave for it. It's the same with smoking. You cannot miss smoking as a pleasure once you have seen through the ridiculous illusion that it could ever be a pleasure. But unlike the roller coaster ride, you can miss smoking for other reasons to do with addiction illusions that create fear and panic. These are the real reasons why you smoke - not the pleasure.

Let me put it to you another way. The pleasure you believe you get when you smoke is a conditioned response. Take the example of a laboratory animal. If you force a dog to smoke for a few weeks or months, it will not become addicted to nicotine. There are two reasons for this. One is that nicotine is not physically addictive, the other is that it doesn't do anything. If you give a dog heroin for a few weeks it will definitely go nuts if you suddenly stop. This is because heroin is physically addictive. However, if you force a dog to smoke just before every meal, the dog will associate the smoking with the pleasure of the meal. So the dog's response to smoking will be the production of saliva and a feeling of pleasure. If you then stop the smoking, because the dog is not intelligent enough to have a whole complex set of other illusions about smoking, it will not miss the smoke before the meal. Not at all. No animal could ever become addicted to nicotine because smoking is simply too obnoxious for any animal to choose to do it and they are not intelligent enough to over ride that with a complex set of illusions.

I must stress at this point that I certainly do not condone animal laboratory experiments and it was not my intent to offend anyone with the previous examples.

Cigarettes taste good

In this section we will look at the belief that smoking has a taste and that taste is good. By the end of the section you will know why this illusion exists and armed with this knowledge you will no longer associate smoking with pleasurable taste sensation.

What do they taste like?

Which cigarettes taste better?

We are born with genetically passed on instincts, developed through millions of years of evolution, or designed by God, or both, that try to tell us when we are eating something that has gone off, or is not good for us, or is potentially poisonous or toxic. Smell and taste are linked and we instinctively know when the meat or milk has gone off, and we don't need to be taught that dung is bad to eat because it actually smells and tastes foul to us.

All cigarettes smell and taste foul because they are toxic and poisonous. So why do they taste nice? Well, they don't, unless you happen to be addicted to tobacco. When any kind of addiction is satisfied there is a physical response, one of which is the production of saliva. Any kind of release of tension produces this response. If you don't have a wee for a good while and you're absolutely bursting, when you actually relieve yourself, saliva is produced in your mouth, as if you were going to eat something. At this point, anything you put in your mouth is

119

going to taste good, or at least, tolerable, even if it actually doesn't taste too good.

We have our animal instincts to tell us what tastes good or bad, but in humans, this is easily over-ridden by learning. We learn to like the taste of things that most animals wouldn't go near - i.e. tandoori chicken masala, Swedish wine, parmesan cheese and marmite. We learn to be disgusted by our own natural body smells. Animals can't understand this because they don't have the learning capacity to over-ride their genetic instinct. Our genetic instincts are very weak and our learning capacity is very strong - in other words, to a human, things don't actually taste good or bad in themselves, it is what we believe that makes things taste good or bad. And humans don't agree with each other. Westerners don't like roast caterpillar with garlic sheep's eyes (which is nutritionally very good for you) and Easterners tend not to get overly excited about pork pie and mushy peas. The point is that it is what we believe that counts - not what actually is. Whether you are an animal, an Easterner or a Westerner, unless you are a nicotine addict, cigarette smoke tastes obnoxious.

There's another reason why cigarettes don't taste nice - eat one, you'll soon find out they don't taste nice at all. So it's the smoke that tastes nice? Well that's not really possible is it. You are not eating the smoke you can only really smell it. But when you are smoking it does feel rather like you are actually eating the smoke. This is because you are experiencing relief from the tension of withdrawal and there is this physical response of saliva being produced in the mouth. It's a similar sensation to eating. It is a learned response. This saliva response occurs not simply just because of relief of tension, it also occurs, to some extent, when you chain smoke because it is a learned physical response. Just like Pavlov's dog and the bell. The smell of the smoke triggers the saliva response so it feels like you are eating and tasting. This didn't happen with the first cigarette. The first cigarette smelt and tasted quite disgusting because to a non-addict, they do taste and smell unpleasant.

Because this is a learned response and because different brands of cigarettes produce slightly different smelling smoke, then when you switch brands, you do get a sense of how awful cigarettes really taste because the learned response is very subtle and accurate, tailored to your usual brand, finely tuned to the usual smell of your usual brand's smoke. Another brand's smoke smells slightly different so the saliva response is not triggered as fully so you get a sense of how cigarettes really taste and smell. That's why you don't like other brands of cigarettes unless they are similar to your own. However, if you are determined to change brands after a while your brain will trigger the learned response to the new brand.

When I smoked ordinary filter tipped cigarettes I couldn't stand roll-ups and I could never imagine liking them, they made my throat hurt. But when I became poor and was forced to get used to them, I enjoyed roll-ups tremendously and thought they tasted really nice. That is, one certain brand of tobacco tasted really nice. I didn't know how anyone could have enjoyed those other brands - they made my throat hurt.

In reality cigarettes taste foul if you eat them. In reality cigarette smoke smells and tastes quite unpleasant. The rest is an illusion. Smokers don't enjoy the taste; they experience relief from the anxiety the last cigarette created. When you are free, you cannot enjoy the taste of a cigarette. There is simply nothing to miss.

After a meal

This section works through many of the reasons why those cigarettes after meals seem to be better than other cigarettes. By the end of the section you will have a very clear and full idea of how this illusion works so that you will not miss them after meals ever again.

But what about those cigarettes after meals? Surely I would miss them? After a meal is when I most enjoy smoking, I'll go nuts if I can't have one after a meal.

There is a collection of reasons why cigarettes after meals seem more enjoyable and more valuable than other cigarettes and why there seems a greater need to smoke at that time. We will look at each factor in turn and bear in mind each reason is connected to every other reason. Becoming aware of every aspect of this illusion is essential for you to be free.

Deprivation

When you eat a meal you do not smoke. You could smoke, but your conscience will not let you do something so disgusting while eating a meal. So whether because of practicalities or conscience, the fact is you can't smoke while eating a meal. You are deprived. With deprivation comes fear. Fear that something might happen to prevent you smoking after the meal. Fear that the cravings may come while you are still eating and cannot smoke. It is not a dramatic thing going on it is a subtle, almost imperceptible feeling. It is not serious it is just one factor, after all you will be able to smoke after you have finished your meal.

Anticipation

You know that by the time you will be able to smoke you will be feeling uncomfortable withdrawals. At the start of a meal you always anticipate uncomfortable withdrawal. This can be conscious or sub-conscious. You know there will be feelings of need by the end of the meal. By then, most of the nicotine in your brain will be gone and you will be experiencing withdrawal. Remember what withdrawal is - the slight feeling of something missing that turns into anxiety then panic when it becomes a conscious thought.

You anticipate smoking after the meal. There are a number of things happening in this anticipation. Firstly, there is anticipation that you will smoke and then feel relief from the withdrawals: that is, an anticipated relief from the fear of withdrawals. This cigarette will seem better than others, because it will give relief from the fear that comes with the deprivation.

Secondly, there is anticipation that this cigarette will taste nicer than other cigarettes. It will seem to taste nicer because you already have a mouthful of saliva from eating the food, and this will get rid of the nasty taste better and more quickly than at other times. Quite often people need a drink to really enjoy a cigarette. Drinks work in the same way. The taste of the drink will help take away the nasty taste of the cigarette smoke and the drink will induce the production of saliva to take away the nasty smoke residue in your mouth. This all goes to creating the insane illusion that cigarette smoke has a nice taste.

Most smokers make sure they have a cigarette just before a meal so that they are stocked up with nicotine. This ensures that the suffering of withdrawal won't come for a while and they can enjoy some of the meal without fear or anxiety of withdrawal. To smokers, having a meal seems to make a cigarette more necessary and therefore more enjoyable at the end of the meal. During the meal a smoker is deprived. Ordinarily, this is no big deal. When a smoker gets in a taxi or on a bus where they can't smoke for a while there is no problem in handling this because there is nothing can be done about it. But having a meal is different because the smoker can hurry the meal along, or even not eat it all and get to the cigarette earlier. Meals necessitates a period of deprivation which causes the anticipation of withdrawal and the relief from that withdrawal.

Surroundings

When people are eating they tend to be in a good space mentally and emotionally. They are on a break from work or chores. It is a time of relaxation and enjoyment. A bit of treasured space in the day when all you have to do is eat. Plus you can take part in other pleasurable activities such as listening to music, reading, watching TV or conversing with friends or family. On the whole, meal times are times when people enjoy themselves with no feelings of guilt or shame or urgency. You are relaxed, filled, fulfilled, perhaps in good company, and feeling safe and secure and OK. On the whole. This wonderful

125

space is spoilt however if you are a nicotine addict. The full pleasure of the experience is denied to a nicotine addict because of that slight feeling of emptiness brought on as the nicotine from the previous cigarette leaves the brain. This slight withdrawal feeling is amplified because everything else is so good in this particular space and moment. The slight feeling of loss seems greater now because everything else is so enjoyable and filling in a physical, psychological and emotional sense. The one disturbance on the scene (withdrawal) tends to stand out like a sore thumb in this particular space and moment. So naturally, the cigarette that relieves this seems to do so more effectively than cigarettes at other times. Because you are already relaxed and enjoying yourself, the relief from withdrawal and anxiety also seems more enjoyable now. The need for the cigarette is greater therefore the cigarette seems more enjoyable. So now there are three different and connected factors making the cigarette after a meal seem more needed and enjoyable.

A period of deprivation.

Anticipation of withdrawal and relief from withdrawal.

Being in a comfortable space that is spoilt by withdrawal.

Being filled/eating association

When you have a meal you are filling an empty space in your stomach. There is a strong feeling of safety and security and completeness that accompanies the filling of this empty space.

126

The initial feeling that accompanies the empty space, i.e. hunger, is an uncomfortable feeling and eating relieves the discomfort. Does this whole process of filling and relieving an uncomfortable empty space remind you of anything at all? Yes of course, drug addiction. The feelings that accompany hunger and nicotine withdrawal are very similar. There is a sense of emptiness that triggers feelings of loss and deprivation and grief etc. This leads to anxiety and irritability. The effects of withdrawal and hunger can be quite extreme if a person is deprived of food or a drug. People will break moral boundaries to satisfy the cravings. Starving people will eat things they wouldn't normally consider eating, and they will steal or even kill to do so. Drug addicts will do almost anything to relieve the feelings of withdrawal, such as lie and cheat, steal and beg, and walk miles in the snow and rain in the middle of the night to get to the all-night garage. Eating and smoking are very similar in some quite fundamental ways. At the end of the meal, the whole eating a meal experience has been wasted if the addict cannot fill the other emptiness with the drug. A nicotine addict can't really feel satisfied at the end of the meal while the emptiness of withdrawal is still there. A cigarette is a must at this point because it's not possible to feel filled and satisfied by the meal until the other craving has been satisfied. Also, the fact that one craving has been satisfied makes the other craving for the drug seem even worse than it is normally. And so there's been deprivation, anticipation, completeness in the moment and now another filled emptiness all joining together to make the emptiness and uncomfortableness of withdrawal all the more up front and acute. That's a lot going on there and yes, there is still more to come.

But before we continue on to the next factor relating to this particular aspect of nicotine addiction I would like to digress, because it is important to know the essential difference between withdrawal and hunger as well as the similarities.

Think back to a time when you were hungry and you were anticipating eating one of your favourite meals. For me, this is stuffed peppers followed by lasagne at a particular restaurant in Huddersfield. Mmmm mmmm. They give you a lot and by the end of the meal I'm absolutely stuffed. In fact, when I'm stuffed the idea of eating stuffed peppers has no attraction at all and the leftovers on the plate seem quite disgusting, much the same as an ashtray to a smoker. You know those wildlife programmes on TV when you see the group of lions eating away at their kill. Eventually, when they have eaten their fill, they walk away and leave the rest for the scavengers. They don't do this out of kindness or a sense of social responsibility; it's just that they have had enough. They don't guard the meat because animals live in the moment and at this particular time the meat doesn't seem to them to be anything worth guarding - they simply don't want it, they have had enough and it no longer has any attraction for them. Just as the leftovers of my stuffed peppers have no attraction for me. So there is a point of hunger, uncomfortableness and craving, followed by being satisfied and filled. This is the same as addiction, but the bit after it, i.e. not wanting any more, not finding the prospect of more food attractive, even feeling sick about the very idea of eating any more, this is where the similarity between hunger and addiction ends. No matter how many cigarettes you smoke the emptiness will never be satisfied. Yet another smoke never seems unattractive or sick making. In Narcotics Anonymous they say at every meeting that "one is too many and a thousand never enough". This is the nature of addiction. There is never enough. That emptiness can never really be filled. An addict spends their lives partially filling an emptiness that cannot be filled.

Drug addiction progressively gets worse. More and more of the drug is needed over time to have the same effect of relief. The longer you experience the addiction the more sensitive you are to the effects and nature of the drug so the more powerful the whole experience becomes, the more powerful the addiction, the need and the fear. The other reason is that drug addiction is linked to basic emotional fear and insecurity. This link to core issues within a person's psyche is another aspect of addiction that contributes in a more powerful way than just physical withdrawal to the ever increasing need and dependence on more and more. This is why the normal cycle of hunger and eating becomes an illness in many people. People do eat addictively and become ill with obesity and die early as a result. With a normal hunger response the essential difference is that hunger can be satisfied, while addiction cannot.

Consistency

The final reason why those cigarettes after meals seem better than others at other times of the day is to do with the consistency of the conditions and outcome. Every time you have a meal there is deprivation and anticipation. Every time there is the feeling of being filled by the food and then the cigarette. Every time the outcome is a double dose of relief from hunger and relief from withdrawal. It is always the same, therefore it is reliable, it becomes familiar and secure and comfortable and safe. Some of the important things we seek in life – comfort, security, familiarity and safety. The result is always consistent and this consistency reinforces the belief that a cigarette after a meal is better seem even more real. In reality, the cigarette still tastes foul but the illusion is so strong because of all these factors. Thus giving up after meal times seems more difficult than other times. It seems to a smoker that even after giving up you will always miss those cigarettes after meals. This is simply not true. It is not true because when you are not fooled by the illusions, when you can see all the factors that create the illusion, that cigarette after the meal has no appeal or attraction whatsoever. The truth is cigarettes taste foul, they spoil a meal. The truth is if you are not withdrawing you cannot get relief and the feeling of being filled by smoking a cigarette, you only get an obnoxious taste in your mouth and some dizziness and feeling sick. If you are not withdrawing you cannot benefit from the illusion no matter how strong that illusion is. Smokers who are free, and there are millions of us, do not ever desire or miss a cigarette after a meal. A cigarette would simply spoil the moment because there is no illusion of need or pleasure.

Now please say out loud six times – just do it!

***These** feelings and this confusion will pass whether I smoke or not.*
*These feelings and this confusion **will** pass whether I smoke or not.*
*These feelings and this confusion will **pass** whether I smoke or not.*
*These feelings and this confusion will pass **whether** I smoke or not.*
*These feelings and this confusion will pass whether **I** smoke or not.*
*These feelings and this confusion will pass whether I smoke **or not**.*

Concentration

In this section we will work through the illusion that smoking helps concentration. By the end of this section you will work through this illusion so that you do not fear being unable to concentrate when you are free.

Smoking helps me concentrate.

If you are a nicotine addict - yes it does. This is not an illusion. It is actually true. Smoking does help a nicotine addict to concentrate. So how does it manage to do this? What exact processes are going on that help smokers concentrate better by smoking?

When you need to concentrate on something, you eliminate distractions so that nothing disturbs your concentration. You sit at your desk, or in front of the TV about to watch your favourite programme. You make sure the lights are just right. You make sure the dog/cat/kids are fed and happy so they won't disturb you. You take off or put on any shoes and clothes in order to feel comfortable. You make yourself a drink before starting. You make sure the room is the right temperature. You make sure you have enough cigarettes so you don't have to find any more when you are busy concentrating. You may even unhook the phone. Basically you are eliminating potential disturbances that will interrupt your concentration.

You eliminate being disturbed by too much or too little light.
You eliminate being disturbed by people and animals.

You eliminate being disturbed by tight fitting or itchy clothing.
You eliminate being disturbed by thirst or hunger.
You eliminate being disturbed by the phone.
You eliminate being disturbed by excessive heat or cold.

Part of being able to concentrate is to control your surroundings by eliminating potential sources of disturbance. This is not the whole story however. The other and probably more important aspect of concentration is the ability to focus your mind. Hands up anyone who's played on an arcade game in an amusement arcade at the seaside, such as racing or shooting or flying or tennis. You are in a draughty smelly place that is always too hot or cold, wearing uncomfortable shoes and there are kids and noise and mayhem all around you. Despite all these disturbances you still manage to focus your mind to the point where you are oblivious to everything around you and guess what, you don't even need a cigarette to help you concentrate for this brief time. This of course is an extreme example of intense mind focusing for a limited time. My point is that concentration is about focusing your mind and this is helped, when you need to concentrate for more that just a brief time, by controlling or eliminating potential sources of disturbance. Those potential sources of disturbance that you cannot eliminate, i.e. the phone might ring, are acceptable and you can still concentrate because it isn't ringing right now, it is only a potential disturbance.

There is one source of disturbance however, that a nicotine addict cannot control. That deep, sub-conscious nagging feeling that something is missing. That little bit of anxiety set off by something that was there and is now gone that all nicotine addicts suffer about fifteen minutes after the last cigarette. Unfortunately, all the usual distractions have just been eliminated. This is something inside ourselves that we cannot eliminate - except by replacing the nicotine. As soon as we light the cigarette we can concentrate again. Not as soon as the nicotine is replaced. In reality the feeling of loss that triggers the anxiety is too slight to bother us enough to break our concentration. It is the anxiety it triggers that breaks our concentration. The nicotine doesn't have to actually be replaced, we just have to satisfy our anxiety. The illusion then is that smoking helps us concentrate. Our last cigarette put nicotine in us and set us up for the anxiety creating feeling of loss that disturbs our concentration. We light another cigarette to eliminate the anxiety. Even the threat of disturbance breaks our concentration. We know that when we put this cigarette out we will soon be disturbed again. So we chain smoke. Sometimes discovering we have two cigarettes lit at the same time.

Smoking helps you concentrate because the processes related to nicotine addiction makes concentration very difficult. Smoking does not help a non-addict, or an ex-addict to concentrate. It could only ever do what it does to smokers all the time; make it very difficult to concentrate. When you are free, a cigarette can no more help you concentrate than the average road drill directly outside your window.

It is easy to see how the physical addiction process creates the illusion that smoking helps concentration. There is another very strong element to this illusion that you need to be aware of. We have grown up with its message from TV and films and other smokers. We were receiving this unquestioned illusion through these sources when we were little children, when we were forming our core beliefs. We have grown up with the message that smoking helps concentration for years and years before we ever smoked ourselves. Why on earth and how on earth could we have ever questioned this clever, subtle shared illusion? We are not stupid or thick or deluded. This is not our fault. At least now we know, so we don't have to suffer from this illusion society and addiction gave us. We now know the truth. Nicotine addiction can only ever obstruct genuine concentration, it can never help it.

Smoking helps you relax

In this section we will look at the illusion that smoking helps relaxation, particularly if you are a nervous person. We will also look at how the contradictory illusion, that smoking helps to wake you up, has arisen. By the end of this section you will have greater insight into how conflicting illusions create the addiction trap and you will have seen the nonsense of these illusions so you can no longer suffer from them.

What physically happens when you light up?
How cigarettes help you relax.
How to relax when free.

When you smoke a cigarette there are a complex set of thoughts and feelings going off that triggers physical responses. First there is anticipation. Once you make the decision to have a cigarette you anticipate some kind of benefit such as *"you'll enjoy it"*, *"it tastes nice"*, *"it'll help me concentrate"* or *"it'll help me relax"*. The anticipation is sometimes slight, sometimes much greater. If the anticipation is particularly powerful adrenaline is triggered into your system producing a feeling of even greater excitement. When you light up and inhale the toxic fumes, your brain and body react as they would naturally to any poison gas attack, and produce more adrenaline. This causes all kinds of physical reactions: increased blood pressure; increased heart rate, and increased perspiration; temporary suspension of digestion, and relaxation of the bladder. There is also some head dizziness and slight nausea as your system reacts to the poisonous substances in the inhaled smoke.

This is what really, actually happens. All these physical responses kick off in reaction to the suicidal inhalation of toxic fumes. How on earth did we ever get to the saddest illusion of all, that smoking helps you relax?

Here's how. As we know, the feeling that something is missing when the nicotine from the last cigarette is flushed away creates feeling of anxiety, irritability, loss, grief, insecurity, discomfort. When a smoker is trying to relax, it's virtually impossible to relax until the nicotine is replaced. Once it is replaced, there is a sense of relief from the awful insecurity and the whole process results in the illusion that smoking helps you relax.

Imagine, you have finished your work or chores or whatever and this is your time for you. You have your shoes off, your comfortable clothes on. You're in your favourite chair with your coffee or tea or lager or chocolate. You are watching TV or listening to music or reading or whatever. This is your time and space for relaxation. But there is a little nagging feeling that something is missing. The fact that all other barriers to relaxation have been sorted out makes this little nagging feeling that something is missing seem even bigger than it actually is. That there are no other disturbances going on vying for your attention means that you can focus on the little nagging feeling that there is something missing, and it very quickly consumes you until you get a cigarette. Most smokers avoid this period of discomfort and disturbance of relaxation by smoking immediately and they do this by believing that smoking helps them relax. This actually is not far from the truth. The truth is a nicotine addict cannot relax without smoking. Smoking does all kinds of things to a person's body and brain, but relaxation is not one of them; it's simply that any kind of genuine relaxation is out of the question for a nicotine addict.

I once tried this method of meditation. I got a book and it took you through various stages to help you acquire the skills of deep meditation. The first week you just had to sit and be still. You had to learn how to relax your body and be still. I could manage about twenty minutes providing I'd topped up well with nicotine before-hand, but doing beyond twenty minutes was not possible for me because my thoughts turned to smoking and once that happened there was no chance of really relaxing. Having been a smoker for many years I had no way of knowing what genuine relaxation was. My closest experience of relaxation depended on chemical relief from chemical induced withdrawal – i.e. smoking. Genuine relaxation was not part of my life. One of my fears about being free was that I didn't know how to relax. I couldn't imagine being relaxed without the use of nicotine. My imagination could not take me beyond withdrawal and into the world of freedom. I wondered whether it would ever be possible to really feel relaxed and comfortable without smoking, even though I was aware that the relaxation I had with smoking was not really genuine relaxation.

Today I am free. I am not a nicotine addict. When I relax today it is a genuine peace. When I rest today it is real rest and it refreshes me. My rest and relaxation is of far better quality because it is not dependent on a drug and I am not suffering the physical responses brought on by the suicidal inhalation of toxic fumes. More importantly I am not suffering from the guilt and shame of harming myself; my relaxation today is nurturing and empowering. I am not suffering from the fear and tension of future heart disease and lung cancer and thrombosis. I have a clearer conscience and I am proud that I made the effort to love myself enough to face my fear of freedom and to have the courage to question my ignorance and challenge my belief system. You today are having the courage and self love to make the effort for yourself and to face your fear and challenge your beliefs. You can look forward to a quality of relaxation you cannot currently imagine, one that non-smokers take for granted. You can experience relaxation with gratitude and a deep appreciation because of years of denial.

I am a nervous person

Some people label themselves as being nervous people or as having problems with their nerves. Following on from this come the beliefs that smoking helps to calm those nerves or provide some confidence or respite from the nervous feeling. This can be quite complicated because some people think that their anxiety is a result of a nervous disposition and that this nervous disposition is a physical problem with the nerves in the body, so the whole issue can get very complicated and another hundred books could be written to dealt entirely with this issue. Labelling oneself a nervous person or suffering from nerves or having a nervous disposition usually has with it a very complex set of beliefs and thought patterns that support addiction illusions.

Once you have been diagnosed as a nervous person or as suffering from nerves by yourself, a doctor or relatives, then that label can be used as an excuse to smoke every single cigarette you ever smoke. The cause of this decision can be very complex.

It may be as a result of shame, low self-esteem, inappropriate guilt, or a mixture of all three. It can even stem from a physical problem that was once experienced, such as a shock that has never really been recovered from. Situations in life, particularly difficult situations can trigger off the feelings experienced in the initial shock which in turn can trigger off all sorts of other emotions like shame, guilt and anxiety that have nothing to do with the present situation.

If you consider yourself a nervous person or suffer from nerves, although I have used the term 'label' I do not mean to demean you or your problems in any way whatsoever. By using the term 'label' I am not trying to lessen the problems or to put you down, nor am I trying to suggest that you choose it rather than it just happening. I am simply saying that once that label is applied it is an excuse to smoke and becomes a reason to smoke. The good news about this is that choosing to smoke because you are a nervous person or giving in to smoking because you suffer from nerves has a very simple answer. You can only use cigarettes if you believe they help calm your nerves, i.e. if they help you relax or if they help you cope with life or anxiety in some way. If you honestly look this belief squarely in the eye you can only see that a cigarette cannot help you cope with anything and can never calm your nerves or help you relax.

Does smoking help calm nerves? If so, how does it help calm nerves? I cannot answer the question, how does smoking help calm nerves, because it would be like trying to answer the question, how does playing football repair a leaking tap? It doesn't, and it can't. There is no way of connecting the calming of nerves with smoking a cigarette. I can, however, show you that disturbing your nervous system and creating anxiety is something that smoking does with great efficiency. In fact, the inhalation of any toxic fumes would certainly have an impact on your nervous system by inducing the body to kick off its defence system. This would trigger the adrenaline that would make your heart beat faster, your breathing quicker; there would be more oxygen and energy going to your muscles that could create some trembling. As you can see, it is very easy to describe how a cigarette can trigger off nerves.

That's just on a physical level. On an emotional level, if you believe that a cigarette helps you relax then you can also believe it helps calm your nerves. Since that is your belief then it will work for you as it has done thousands of times in the past and for many years. The fact that it is in reality nonsense, the fact that it is an illusion, a mistaken belief, doesn't lessen its effect. While you are in that illusion it will still seem to calm your nerves. The main illusion is connected to the physical addiction itself: nicotine leaving the brain creates a sense of loss that quickly turns into anxiety and even panic attacks that can be mistaken for bad nerves. It is the addiction itself that sets up that anxiety, the last cigarette you smoked. It has nothing to do with you being a nervous person or suffering from bad nerves. This is extra, on top of any existing condition. Smoking creates anxiety on a consistent daily basis regardless of whether or not you have a pre-existing nervous condition. That is how the addiction itself works and it is completely separate to any nervous disposition. The only way to make sure that you keep experiencing this added, extra anxiety on a daily basis is to smoke. If you stop smoking you could not experience the constant anxiety the addiction gives you, neither can you experience relief of that anxiety by smoking because once the nicotine is out of your system you cannot experience relief from the anxiety the last cigarette set up for you.

In the past, each time you have smoked a cigarette and got relief from the anxiety the last cigarette created, the illusion that the cigarette helped calm your nerves seemed very real. It seemed very real thousands of times over a period of many years so you have had no cause to question or doubt it. But just because it is a very good trick and just because that trickery and illusion has been reinforced so many times over all this time does not make it true. The truth is that smoking creates anxiety and can create problems with your nervous system because it is a drug and it is full of toxins and poisons. The other truth is that smoking can never calm your nerves or relax you in any way, it is impossible. The truth is that if you believe it calms your nerves then it will seem to do that but it can't actually do that. Becoming free from this addiction could contribute to a partial or full recovery from any nervous disposition; continuing smoking cannot help at all.

Smoking helps to wake me up

The very first person I helped to become free in my clinics had the illusion that he needed to smoke to wake up on a morning. Having proved that smoking keeps you awake and doesn't help you relax then surely it must help you to wake up instead. That first dizzy buzz on a morning gets you out of your sleepy daze. Let's look at this illusion.

If you are Mr or Mrs Groggy in the morning then there are a number of things you can do to wake yourself up. You can

141

throw some water over your head, run into the wall, get a friend to slap your face hard a few times or whip you with a leather whip (oooer!) or you could inhale some toxic fumes into your lungs. The choice is yours, personally I like the whip, I just don't have a friend who is willing to do it. But seriously, some people are bright and breezy first thing and some are slow and groggy. I am of the latter persuasion. I have never been bright and breezy in the morning and I have always had an intense dislike of those people who jump out of bed ready to face the world. I thought that smoking was one of the causes of me being Mr Groggy at the start of each day and I was looking forward to becoming a cheerful chappie at the crack of dawn when I was free from this addiction. My morning grogginess has not improved much since becoming free. I have to admit it has improved a little, but it was bound to be a bit better simply because I am healthier and cleaner and I have more oxygen floating around in my blood because my lungs are more efficient. But essentially I am still Mr Groggy, or at least Mr slightly less groggy but still pretty groggy on a morning. I am still looking for a friend with a whip.

It does nothing for you

In this section we will take a brief look at how the collection of addiction illusions can blind people from the truth. By the end of this section you will clearly see how illusions about smoking keep people trapped and how seeing those illusions sets you free.

If it's true, that the only pleasure to be gained from smoking is the relief from the withdrawals then there is simply no problem in not smoking, just as there is no problem in not putting on a tight belt for the pleasure of relief in taking it off again. So in order to get to the stage of knowing that relief from withdrawal is the only pleasure, we have to be sure that this is in fact true.

Alcohol makes me feel woozy and dizzy and I lose my inhibitions and I feel confident. Marijuana makes me feel giggly and I experience freedom from worry and my sensations of colour and taste are enhanced. Acid makes me feel very sensitive all over my body and I feel really randy. What does nicotine do? Absolutely nothing whatsoever! Nothing. I don't feel drunk or stoned. It doesn't make me feel particularly randy or confident or excited. I used to think I got pleasure from smoking. I used to think I did it because it tasted good. Lots of things taste better that I wouldn't dream of having forty times a day every single day for years and years. I used to think it helped me relax. The truth is that it stopped me from being able to properly relax. I used to think smoking helped me concentrate, until I found out that smoking stopped me from being able to really concentrate. I used to think that smoking gave me confidence and made me a grown-up until I realised it is a stupid and childish thing to do

143

and in reality I never respected any other smoker or even myself for being a smoker. I used to think smoking helped me cope with things that life has a habit of throwing at you. The truth became apparent that smoking was a way of avoiding life, escaping from feelings and inflicting self destruction rather than any way of coping with anything in a healthy, positive or strong way. All the reasons I had to smoke were taken away and replaced with truth. The only pleasure or reason to smoke that I had left was the relief a smoke gave me from the fear of the withdrawal the last smoke set up for me. Even that last reason was removed when the truth was given to me that the withdrawal and the fear of withdrawal would pass whether I smoked or not.

TRUTH

WITHDRAWAL AND THE FEAR OF WITHDRAWAL MUST PASS WHETHER YOU SMOKE OR NOT.

This last piece of truth shattered the last remnant of reason I had to smoke. It is such an important thing to know. Withdrawal and the fear of withdrawal must pass whether you smoke or not. They will pass if you smoke, they will pass if you don't.

If you suffer withdrawal or fear of withdrawal - because you can't actually suffer withdrawal from nicotine because it is so slight, - then the withdrawal may pass quicker if you have a smoke. The trouble is, this is a lie. Withdrawals pass much, much quicker if you don't have a smoke. By smoking you are still suffering from the fear of withdrawal years later, whereas by not smoking you are ensuring you will never suffer from the fear of withdrawal again. Withdrawal and the fear of withdrawal can only be kept and repeated over and over again if you smoke.

TRUTH

WITHDRAWAL AND THE FEAR OF WITHDRAWAL CAN ONLY BE KEPT AND REPEATED OVER AND OVER AGAIN IF YOU SMOKE.

If you do not smoke, you cannot continue suffering from withdrawal and the terrible fear of withdrawal, it is impossible.

TRUTH

IF YOU DO NOT SMOKE, YOU CANNOT CONTINUE SUFFERING FROM WITHDRAWAL AND THE TERRIBLE FEAR OF WITHDRAWAL, IT IS IMPOSSIBLE.

Ex Smokers

In this section we will look at different types of ex-smokers and their influence. Specifically we will work through the common thoughts and beliefs ex-smokers have that can affect you when you stop smoking. There is an exercise to help you identify the hidden messages behind the things they say. By the end of this section you will have a deeper understanding of what genuine freedom from this addiction really is so you can have a genuine and permanent freedom.

Trying to become free is beset with traps and slippy bits and big holes you can fall down. The path to freedom has some very subtle, negative influences that can cause you to doubt and waiver and suffer. A major booby trap on this path can be the ex-smoker.

Recent ex-smokers who are having problems quite often talk about it and share their problems with others. This can be very helpful in some cases because it helps them to feel supported rather than alone. Ex-smokers who aren't particularly having problems with it tend not to need to share what they are going through so much. Long term ex-smokers who are having problems will often share their problems with anyone who mentions they are stopping smoking, but though they will try to do it in an encouraging way, generally you still get to hear about their problems despite them having given up smoking some time ago. You hear things like, *"I still get cravings"* or *"pangs, especially after meals"* or *"I still think about it sometimes."* This of course boils down to the fact they are not free, they have just given up smoking. Long term ex-smokers who are free tend either to not mention it at all or encourage you by telling you they gave up and are fine. The difference is not so much the message, but that ex-smokers who are not free tend to offer their advice without needing much or any encouragement whereas ex-smokers who are genuinely free only tend to mention it if they are directly asked. The upshot of all this is that smokers who are thinking about giving up are mostly inundated with the messages of those ex-smokers who are not free and who are having problems. This can create the illusion that it is never really possible to be completely happy not smoking once you have been a smoker. Doubt about the future creeps in and this creates anxiety and fear and adrenaline and a greater need to smoke now to be rid of these feelings/withdrawals.

During my long, long struggle to be free I asked one of my friends who I knew was free, how he did it. He told me his story that basically went like this: he experienced a moment in time where he couldn't see the point in doing it any more, and he never smoked since and never experienced any withdrawals whatsoever. He saw the truth, and the truth made him free. He doesn't miss smoking, he sees no pleasure in smoking and he has not required it as any sort of prop. What really freaked me out about his attitude was the sheer solidness and certainty and peace he had about the issue. There simply was no suffering or doubt or sense of loss. I couldn't personally identify with any of it. But it was powerful and real to me. I had to admit at the time that I was aware of ex-smokers like that, who had no issue about it at all. I was jealous of them and angry at God/life that I had not been given such a gift as this, especially when I thought of all the effort and time I had spent trying to stop. If we are honest, most of us know at least one or two ex-smokers who are genuinely free. They don't talk about it unless specifically asked to, and what they do have to say doesn't help us at all because we can't identify with it. We can't understand.

The long term ex-smokers who are not free, on the other hand, we understand with no problem at all. They may not be smoking but they are still in the same trap we are in. They tell us about their problems so we know who they are and we don't have to ask them anything. Simply hint that you might be thinking about considering stopping smoking and they tell you how they went through hell doing it and they still suffer now and again, especially after meals or when they have accidents or shocks etc etc etc. . . They still miss cigarettes. They feel deprived of a pleasure. They are choosing to suffer rather than give in to the cravings because they are so strong. What's confusing to us and to them is that in another breath they say that once they were over the first few days/weeks/months, it became very easy. They are still the victim of addiction beliefs and illusions. They still believe the illusions of pleasure, and prop and need. But the real truth is, it is easy not to smoke. Some of them will continue to suffer now and again, some of them will become free over time and some of them will smoke again no matter how long they have stopped. These ex-smokers who are not really free are the ones to be wary of. Their expressed messages reach deep into the heart of our addiction and can cause us to waiver and doubt and suffer. They can't make us smoke, we have to take responsibility for that. But they can cause us doubt, anxiety and fear. The fear is, "*Will I suffer or crave like that? Will I miss smoking like them? Will I miss the pleasure like they do? Will I feel the need at difficult times like them?*"

You have to choose now, whether these people are a gift or a threat. As a trapped smoker trying to stop smoking there is no choice - these people are to be feared and avoided. As a freedom seeker you have a choice. You can choose the truth. The truth is these people are a useful tool to us. They bring us issues and aspects of the dysfunctional beliefs and illusions so that we are given an opportunity to affirm and strengthen our new belief system and to further destroy our own illusions. They are beacons of light to us: the truth is, not smoking is easy and very possible even if you are still the victim of the beliefs and delusions that is addiction. They prove to us that stopping is so easy you can still do it even if you are still trapped in addiction. Not only that, they challenge our new truths so that we are given an opportunity to re-affirm that smoking is not a pleasure, it doesn't help us cope and we don't miss that awful ball and chain, the prison that is addiction.

We don't want to be like them, we don't have to be like them and we are genuinely grateful we are not like them. They provide us with an opportunity to experience gratitude. A wonderful feeling to be enjoyed whenever the opportunity presents itself.

If you want to be free, these still suffering ex-smokers are a gift and tool to help you on your path. I don't mean you actively seek them out or argue with them. You don't need them to be free. They are simply an aid in the process whenever they arise. If you want to stay stuck in your addiction live in fear of them. Avoid them. Don't address the issues and doubts they present. Run away and stay stuck in fear and addiction. It's a straight choice that only you can make.

Let's look at how this process actually works. When an ex-smoker says, *"I found it fairly easy once I got through the first three weeks and now I only have a twinge very occasionally like when something bad happens or sometimes after meals."* What they are saying is:-

It takes three weeks of suffering. You will always suffer now and again, so you can never really be free.

The very next thought you have about it is your choice and responsibility. You have doubt and say, "Maybe they are right." Or you can identify that they are not free and you can immediately remember the ex-smokers who are free and identify yourself with them. Then you can add emotion to strengthen this thought by feeling pity and understanding for them.

1.   Identify this person is not free.
2.   *That's not me - I'm like the free ones*
3.   Pity them

Every time you go though that process in your mind you can become more free. In that way you are choosing to be different to that person who is clearly struggling or having doubts and problems. Now that you are not in their camp you can take an objective view of the things they are saying. This will give you a choice regarding what you think and how you feel. Every issue they have is an opportunity for you to address that issue in your own mind. For example, if they say, *"I am taking it one day at a time"*, then you can identify that this is not something a free ex-smoker would say. When you have identified that this person is not free, then you can imagine what a free ex-smoker would have to say about that issue. So a free person might say, *"I've stopped for good and I am not struggling through one day at a time."* This then becomes the opinion you can choose to adopt. In this way, the messages of a struggling ex-smoker are opportunities to strengthen your own belief system that keeps you free.

Mr Doubt & Mr Free

Here is an exercise for you to do. Take a sheet of paper and draw a 'Mr Doubt' face on one side and a 'Mr Free' face on the other side.

Underneath the drawings you will be writing what each one of them might say. Below is a list of things that Mr Doubt, the struggling ex-smoker, might say. I want you to write that down under your drawing of Mr Doubt, and under Mr Free write down the answer a free person would say. There are no right or wrong answers but you might find you have to first translate what Mr Doubt is actually saying underneath the words. i.e. identify the issue, before you create your answer. Be as creative as you like but try and deal with the issue itself rather than just a clever rebuff. Here is an example:-

Mr Doubt says . . .

I still have pangs now and again- these 'pangs' are slight panic attacks. They are caused by thoughts. Thoughts of need or pleasure associated with smoking. All these thoughts are illusions that this person has not seen through, so although the person has stopped smoking, they are not free from the addiction. This clearly proves that not smoking is easy because these people do it while they still have the illusions that make up the addiction.

Mr Free says . . . *I never have pangs, they stopped when I faced all the illusions.*

I'm taking it one day at a time.

I've stopped for good. I'm not struggling one day at a time.

After you have completed your answers compare them with the answers given below. This exercise is important and it may well take you quite a long time. The more care and time you devote to this the greater will be your benefit. There are no wrong answers because it is an exploration and a learning of a thought process. The more of these you choose to do the better, but it is a long list and it isn't critical that you do absolutely all of them. Pick first those that seem easiest and go on from there to try those that seem harder. Don't cheat by looking at the answers, have a go yourself first. This kind of thing is very helpful because you are doing something in an active way instead of just passively reading. These exercises are designed to change the way you think so that you become free from your addiction. Have a go, devote some time, it is well worth it.

Mr Doubt says . . .

1. *I still have pangs now and again*

2. *Sometimes I could murder a cig*

3. *I miss the ones after meals*

4. *The first three days are the worst*

5. *Once you get past three weeks it gets a lot easier*

6. *Just don't think about it*

7. *I only smoked a bit anyway*

8. *I gave up for two years, then I started again and now I've been stopped for six months*

9. *I put loads of weight on when I stopped*

10. *Once an addict, always an addict*

11. *Even though I have stopped now, I wish I'd never started*

12. *When the cravings come up I just take ten deep breaths and I'm alright*

13. *I hate anyone smoking near me now*

14. *I used nicotine patches*

15. *Just say no whenever you want one*

16. *I stopped for my children*

17. *I just delay having one for five minutes and I keep doing that*

18. *When the cravings come just do something else like walking or washing up.*

Possible answers

Here below are examples of possible answers to each one. Compare and contrast your own answers to these examples so that your conscious mind can explore even further. This exercise is developing a thought pattern that will enable you to stay free for the rest of your life.

Mr Doubt says . . . *Sometimes I could murder a cig*

This is an illusion of pleasure. This person still believes that smoking a cigarette will give them pleasure. They do not know that the only pleasure to be had from smoking is the relief from withdrawal the last cigarette set up. Unfortunately, this person has stopped smoking, so there can be no pleasure from their next cigarette, only a bad taste some nausea and dizziness.

Mr Free says . . . *there is no pleasure, only a bad taste.*

Mr Doubt says . . . *I miss the ones after meals*

This person has no idea whatsoever of the reasons why a smoke after a meal seems more pleasurable. The illusion is still just as powerful despite the fact that this person has given up smoking.

Mr Free says . . . *That's just an illusion, all cigarettes are the same.*

Mr Doubt says . . . *The first three days are the worst*

This person is saying that you feel bad for three days when you give up smoking. Well if you don't know what is going on you are completely lost as to why you are feeling the feelings; if you are unaware of the slight feeling of loss that creates the anxiety that creates the adrenaline that creates the physical symptoms that creates more anxiety and adrenaline and symptoms etc, then you are bound to feel bad. The important point is though, as lost as this person obviously was, even they could not keep all that fear and discomfort, could not stay in that adrenaline cycle for more than just three days. Your body simply will not allow it.

Mr Free says . . . *I suffered hardly at all because I was completely aware of what was going on.*

Mr Doubt says . . . *Once you get past three weeks it gets a lot easier*

You mean you realised at about the three week mark that not smoking was actually easy? Or maybe your illusions were so trusted that you suffered greatly for three whole weeks? Or maybe you got wise to your illusions three weeks later.

Mr Free says . . . *It gets a lot easier the moment you lose your illusions of need and pleasure.*

Mr Doubt says . . . *Just don't think about it*

Impossible! The problem with running away from issues is that they have a nasty habit of coming back to get you being even more powerful for being so long suppressed.

Mr Free says . . . *I have no issues to get me in the future, I don't run away.*

Mr Doubt says . . . *I only smoked a bit anyway*

So you think that smoking less makes any difference. That is an illusion. Whether you smoke two a day or twenty a day you still smoked for the same reasons.

Mr Free says . . . *I smoked loads. How much you smoked doesn't mean a thing.*

Mr Doubt says . . . *I gave up for two years, then I started again and now I've been stopped for six months*

So you are saying that no matter how long a person stops there is still the struggling going on that makes them smoke even after two years? Stopping smoking must be easy if you can struggle all this time, stopping and starting.

Mr Free says . . . *I am not struggling, I am not stopping anything, I am free.*

Mr Doubt says . . . *I put loads of weight on when I stopped*

This person is implying that you put weight on when you stop smoking. You don't put weight on because you stop smoking, you put weight on because you eat more and the older you get the more prone you are to weight gain. This person substituted food for nicotine in order to try and satisfy a hunger (addition) that could never be satisfied. When you know you are not missing out on anything you do not try to fill a space that is not empty. There is no loss to fill.

Mr Free says . . . *I am free from nicotine addiction. I choose how much I eat.*

Mr Doubt says . . . *Once an addict, always an addict*

This person could be saying the truth that once you have been addicted to a particular drug, you only need one use of that drug to become addicted again instantly. That's true. On the other hand, they might be implying that once you have become addicted you struggle with the addiction for the rest of your life. This is only true if you continue to smoke. If you continue to smoke you are struggling with the addiction every day of your life. If you are free you do not struggle, nor would you dream of having even one cigarette.

Mr Free says . . . *I am free. I am not an addict because I am free.*

Mr Doubt says . . . *Even though I have stopped now, I wish I'd never started*

This person is implying that even though they have stopped smoking they are still struggling and that the only way they would not have to struggle is if they had never smoked. Millions of people who are free from nicotine addiction prove this to be completely wrong. There is no struggle unless you still believe in the illusions that make up addiction.

Mr Free says . . . *I am free as if I had never smoked, I have dealt with all the issues.*

Mr Doubt says . . . *When the cravings come up I just take ten deep breaths and I'm alright*

This person is saying that no matter how long you have given up smoking you will continue to suffer cravings. Once again this proves that this addiction has nothing to do with the drug nicotine which this person has not had in their system for a long time, but is solely to do with the illusions they believe.

Mr Free says . . . *Craving is the result of illusions of need or pleasure. I am free from these illusions, I cannot have cravings.*

Mr Doubt says . . . *I hate anyone smoking near me now*

This person is forming a psychological barrier to smoking in their mind. The more disgust at smoking they can generate, the less likely they are to want to smoke, goes the theory. The existing illusions about the need or pleasure may be still there behind this barrier of disgust, the illusions may still be intact and not dealt with.

Mr Free says . . . *I don't need a barrier of disgust, my old illusions have been dealt with.*

Mr Doubt says . . . *I used nicotine patches*

This person thinks that the addiction to nicotine is mainly to do with the drug nicotine, rather than the anxiety and fear and adrenaline.

Mr Free says . . . *I have awareness of the truth about addiction, I am free.*

Mr Doubt says . . . *Just say no whenever you want one*

Has this person ever smoked? Suppressing desire is inviting an explosion in the future. Nobody really ever **wants** to smoke, this is an illusion. When you think you want a cigarette what you are really wanting is relief from the slight feeling of loss the last cigarette created and you need to avoid the forthcoming panic attack you will have if you decide not to have one. Does a smoker ever really want to smoke? Nobody ever wants to smoke, they simply want the effect which in itself is an illusion. Nobody wakes up one day and decides that it would be a good idea if they became an addicted smoker today. It doesn't work like that. People start smoking out of curiosity, believing that they won't get addicted just by trying one or two. Because the actual nicotine withdrawal is so weak they don't even notice it for ages. This makes them confident that they will not get hooked and even if they do it won't be that bad to give up, after all millions of people have given up smoking. This point is true, it is easy to not smoke once the illusions are no longer in place, because the actual nicotine addiction is so weak. Once a person has proved beyond all doubt to their peers that they have had the bottle to smoke then they will give up. Some people, upon finding they cannot give up, decide that this is because they enjoy smoking and they must therefore want to do it. They don't think about the fact that they enjoy all sorts of other things in life that they wouldn't do twenty or thirty times a day every day,

day in day out at enormous cost in money and health. The illusions of "I want to smoke" and "I enjoy smoking" are really excuses. Reasons not to do the work of breaking free from the addiction. People don't really want to smoke, what they want is the effect. The effect being the relief from current withdrawal and future panic. This effect is turned into all the illusions like smoking helps me relax, is a pleasure, helps me concentrate helps me cope and I fall to pieces without it anyway

Mr Free says . . . *I never want to smoke, I never really did. I am free from that illusion.*

Mr Doubt says . . . *I stopped for my children*

This person may be trying to encourage you to stop by shaming you for smoking in front of the children. Maybe this person is ashamed of themselves?

Mr Free says . . . *I became free for me, not for anyone else.*

Mr Doubt says . . . *I just delay having one for five minutes and I keep doing that*

This person is still in the process of stopping. If they are lucky they may stay in the process of stopping for the rest of their lives. They are also implying that they keep having smoking thoughts and feelings and are not working through their issues. Instead they are just delaying the whole thing.

Mr Free says . . . *I am delaying nothing, I am free.*

Mr Doubt says . . . *When the cravings come just do something else like walking or washing up.*

  This person is saying that they still suffer from cravings and therefore you can never really relax without smoking.

Mr Free says . . . *I am free, I don't suffer cravings and I can relax without smoking.*

Smokers who are ok with smoking

In the next two sections we will look at the influence of smokers and how they might affect you when you have stopped. We will look into their problems and motivations. By the end of the section you will know how and how not to handle other smokers when you are free.

Smoker who are ok with smoking have and express a general attitude about the issue that doesn't require them to be upset about it – i.e. *"I enjoy smoking"*, *"It's my only pleasure/vice"* and *"You've got to die of something"* etc etc etc.

It may be that by adopting such a stance and repeating that thought over and over again whenever the issue arises means that they don't suffer from the guilt and shame the rest of us feel for the slavery and self destruction. The fact that such thoughts are insane is not the point. The point is that they are ok with smoking whether we like it or not and whether we agree with it or not.

So let us now once and for all make a decision about this. Is it ok for those people to enjoy their smoking for whatever reason they think or claim they enjoy about it? Is it ok for us to give them permission to do that without suffering like we do? Is it ok for their path to be their path and for our path to be different and our path? Let's make that ok. We are not living their lives and they are not living our life. Let's make s decision once and for all that it is ok for them to be ok about smoking and at the same time it is ok for us to not be ok about smoking or better still, it is ok for us to be ok being smoke free. We have nothing to prove to anyone else and what others choose to do is none of our business.

During the time I was writing this course I worked in an office. I worked for a very large company, so there were a lot of people working there. I worked in the training department and for some reason, in this particular department, most of the people smoked. I had become free by this time and so I had worked through my beliefs about smoking. One of the beliefs that I had worked through was the very silly idea that smoking somehow relieved stress. There came a point when one of the women who worked there announced that she needed to go and have a smoke to relieve her stress. At that point I felt like crying out to her that was nonsense, smoking does not relieve stress at all, it creates stress. It was frustrating to me because I couldn't really start spouting on about things like that without genuinely risking hurting or offending. She had not asked me to help her with her nicotine addiction, it was not my place to say anything and if I had it would have been taken as criticism.

Apart from the frustration that I couldn't say anything I felt tremendous anger that these insane beliefs are so powerful and keep people trapped in this terrible addiction to the point of strokes, heart disease, loss of limbs and death. On top of this, all the people around her were giving support to that insane belief with their knowing, understanding looks and nods and sympathy for her stress. It felt like being in an asylum. There is an expression that says, "Hell is the impossibility of reason" - and that's what it felt like. When you know the truth it is very frustrating to see other people still believing the lies you once believed. You may find that you tend to over-react to such things as I did. Please remember it is not your place to correct people or to try to help them 'see the light'. It is very tempting to do so but if you do you are simply inviting trouble. People have not asked you to do that and they will be offended and they will take it as criticism. There's no point losing any friends or offending colleagues. The real point here that I want to get across is that you might be quite surprised at the power of you emotional reaction in these situations.

Now please say out loud six times – just do it!

These *feelings and this confusion will pass whether I smoke or not.*
These feelings and this confusion **will** *pass whether I smoke or not.*
These feelings and this confusion will **pass** *whether I smoke or not.*
These feelings and this confusion will pass **whether** *I smoke or not.*
These feelings and this confusion will pass whether **I** *smoke or not.*
These feelings and this confusion will pass whether I smoke **or not**.

Other smokers who don't smoke much anyway

Then there are those smokers who do not class themselves as being addicted. They only smoke a few a day and that's ok because that doesn't affect their health. Also there are those who only smoke occasionally when they go out or on special occasions. These kinds of smokers give us a very good example of the power of illusion. When we first tried smoking it tasted pretty foul and there was no real pleasure except the excitement of the risks we took. The adrenaline rush you get as a teenager when you are playing with fire is in itself a pretty intense pleasure. It was not actually the act of smoking that provided us with pleasure. Eventually our minds became trained to give smoking powers of helping us to concentrate, relax and be mature etc when in fact all it was doing was relieving the withdrawal the last cigarette created.

However, the illusions are so powerful about the pleasure and usefulness of smoking in helping us relax etc and the actual physical withdrawals are so slight, it is certainly possible for the 'occasional' smokers to believe they are enjoying and benefiting from the act of smoking. This is what you need to understand. The power of the shared illusion is so strong it is actually possible to enjoy inhaling foul, toxic fumes and genuinely believe you are benefiting in some way.

Toxic Fumes Nice? Why? I BELIEVE

Do you see? If the belief is real, the pleasure is real. If you don't believe, you cannot enjoy. If the illusions are shattered the desire no longer exists. You no longer want to smoke because many of the illusions have already been shattered. You have already lost a lot of your desire to smoke because you have seen through many of the illusions about pleasure and benefits.

So these smokers who smoke occasionally or only a few a day are in effect more gullible than the rest of us. When you come across people who smoke only occasionally, they are simply a good example of the powers of illusion. It is not your job to convert them. They are simply another way for you to accept the power of the illusion so you don't have to beat yourself up for being in it so long yourself.

There are two further issues we need to look at with regard to these kinds of occasional smokers.

Firstly – are they lying?

Secondly – are they addicted?

Some people just out and out lie about this sort of thing to impress other people. I knew a bloke who only smoked when he went out drinking, or so he said. He went out drinking and stayed in drinking rather a lot and he chain smoked while he was drinking.

Other people don't so much out and out lie about it but mislead others by exaggeration or by omission. A good example of that is when people say, "I don't smoke in the house, only when I go out." They omit to inform you that they 'go out' of the house into the garden shed on average fifteen times a day and smoke two cigarettes each time. But this is ok. The only person they are really deceiving is themselves, nobody else really cares anyway.

What about people who claim they only smoke occasionally and they are not addicted? We must look at this issue because part of the lie of addiction is the insane, impossible hope that we can smoke sensibly without it being an addiction. Is there such a thing as sensible smoking? Are there really people who smoke occasionally who are not addicted? Well if their last smoke was sometime last week then they can't still be suffering physical withdrawal. If they are not withdrawing, then they cannot experience the relief from the withdrawals from the next smoke.

That being the case, why are they even bothering to smoke at all? During the course of my smoking career and during the course of writing this course I have tried to question these people to try to pin down why on earth they are smoking if they are not addicted. Here is a typical example.

"Do you smoke?"
"Well off and on, now and again. I just have the occasional cigarette, I'm not addicted."
"Well if you're not addicted why do you bother smoking at all?"
"Just for pleasure really."
"What pleasure?"
"They taste nice, they help me relax."
"So you eat them."
"No."
"So the smoke tastes nice?"
"Well, yeah."
"So what does it taste like?"
"Sort of cool and minty."

This example is extreme. A conversation like this rarely gets that far. They usually run away very quickly when they know their nonsense is going to be questioned. I have to report to you here and now that my limited research has shown that no such people exist. The hopeless, insane dream that all addicts share about being able to use their drug sensibly is exactly that, a hopeless, insane dream.

However, let's just say for arguments sake there are some people, some misguided believers in the illusions, who are genuine. They smoke occasionally, they are not addicted and they smoke because they believe it tastes nice and helps them relax. What have they got to do with us? Is there any chance at all that you are going to be able to smoke occasionally and not be addicted? Well I've got news for you. You were one of those people. In the early days of your smoking you did pretend it did things for you like tasting nice or helping you relax etc and you were not yet addicted. This period of time between your first smoke and full-on constant smoking may have lasted just a few days, a few weeks or a few months. Isn't it possible therefore that for some people this process takes a few years? You see, the reason it takes most of us a few weeks or months is because the physical withdrawal from nicotine is so slight. It is the mental addiction that matters and a mental addiction takes time to develop. It is a set of beliefs that support each other and this takes a little time to kick in because the beliefs are not actually true. So what if your mind cannot accept the lie that smoking is addictive? You might believe that they taste nice and help you relax, many non-smokers believe that, but if you have a mental block to accepting that smoking is addictive then the simple fact of the matter is you will not become addicted until you work through that mental block.

The point is that these genuine, honest, non-addicted, occasional smokers are very rare, usually temporary and it would be extremely unlikely you would have any chance at all of becoming one.

Nicotine substitutes

In this section we will look at the uses of nicotine substitutes. By the end of the section you will have greater insight into the concept of substitution so that you have no doubt or debate about this issue again.

It is a fact that many people have given up smoking and they have been helped by using nicotine substitutes such as gum, patches and inhalers. It is also a fact that many, many more smokers have been unable to give up despite trying these nicotine substitutes time after time. It is also a fact that a large proportion of people who have used nicotine substitutes and have given up, have gone back to smoking weeks months or sometimes even years later. There are no reliable statistics regarding the long term effectiveness of using nicotine substitutes. There are guesses and opinions and advertising hype, but there is no reliable hard data. So the answer to 'do nicotine substitutes work' is I don't know and I don't know anyone who does.

If by the end of reading this course you think there is value in using nicotine substitutes, then you have missed the point. In order to really know this, we need to first examine why and how they could possibly work. The process of becoming free is a journey of working through enough thoughts and beliefs until there is no need or desire left. One part of this process is seeing through the illusion of withdrawal. One very strong illusion is that uncomfortable withdrawal symptoms are suffered for a particular length of time and when your body re-adjusts itself to life without nicotine the withdrawal symptoms subside and eventually disappear. This is an illusion, it is nonsense. No-one's body ever suffers from not having nicotine. Your heart, lungs, liver, hands, feet and toes do not miss nicotine at all and do not adjust at all to getting used to not having nicotine any more. The physical symptoms that you can suffer are as a result of adrenaline brought on by fear. If you believe this nonsense that your body adjusts to lower levels of nicotine then this is what will seem to happen. If you believe that nicotine substitutes will help you get through this patch of withdrawal, then it is possible that they will because that is what you believe. Most people don't really believe all that, so for most people nicotine substitutes don't work.

What happens after the nicotine substitutes? For some people, feeling safe while not smoking for a period of time allows them to see the illusions of the addiction from an outside perspective. They are temporarily relieved from the immediate head mess of fear and anxiety about the addiction. That period of feeling safe while not smoking itself allows pennies to drop about the illusions of addiction, and some of these people become free in much the same way as I am free, as you will be free and as those annoying people who simply stopped smoking one and never suffered a single second of so-called withdrawal are free.

People using nicotine substitutes believe that there will be less discomfort. It tips the balance for them in that they believe they won't feel too bad because the nicotine is being replaced. Since they believe this they don't feel too bad - just enough to stop smoking. They then feel as if they are getting somewhere and they can feel quite liberated when they suddenly discover the terrible truth that, providing you are not full of fear, not smoking is actually dead easy. They believe that their ability to not smoke is due to the nicotine patches and aren't they a wonderful thing. If a belief in nicotine patches, gum, dummy cigarettes, acupuncture, hypnotism or Indian Head Massage helps to alleviate your fear just enough to not smoke for long enough to realise it is easy then my attitude is 'go for it'.

However, there is a risk. Once you have got over your initial fears and have got some smoke-free time under your belt and have realised that not smoking is easy, then only three things can happen. Either you then go on to address each illusion you had about smoking and deal with it; you just continue suffering now and again feeling as though you are missing out; or those illusions get you back smoking. Those annoying people who just stopped one day and suffered not at all did so because they saw no further point in continuing to smoke. They had seen through their illusions while they were still smoking. This is what this course is helping you to do. But some people stop smoking first, using substitutes or hypnotism or whatever, then they either see through the illusions because they are free from the active addiction or they don't and so continue to suffer or smoke again. Either way, the bottom line is you either see through your illusions about smoking and become free or you don't. If you don't you will either suffer for the rest of your life, or go back to smoking, or have a period of suffering before you go back to smoking.

It's a habit - habits are hard to break

In this section we will look at the concept of 'habit' and what it means and how this concept can turn into an addiction trap. By the end of this section you will see that it is easily possible for you to become free from this habit.

You may have a thought that smoking is a habit and habits are hard to break. Some habits require effort to break and some don't. It may be that you have cornflakes every morning habitually but when you go on holiday you may suddenly have something else for breakfast and you find that the habit of cornflakes wasn't difficult to break at all. Some habits you used to have when you were younger, such as biting your nails, may have disappeared all by themselves. The term 'habit' has various connotations depending upon the context.

Let's establish what we mean by habit. I put my socks on every morning but I don't consider that to be a habit. I brush my teeth each day, but I don't call that a habit, I could give that up no problem. We tend to call something we find difficult to give up a 'habit'. It is usually when something is difficult to give up that we label it a habit. There is another aspect to labelling something a habit. I eat several times a day, and I would find that difficult to give up, but I don't call it a habit. If I ate obsessively and became obese, then I would call it a habit. So habits, to become labelled as being a habit have to firstly be difficult to give up and they have to be bad for us in some way. Sometimes, people refer to having good habits, such as cleaning the bath after use, but that's not difficult to give up so it's not the sort of habit we are concerned with, although there are people who clean obsessively and do find it hard to give up and it is a problem in their lives.

When you define smoking as a habit, you use the concept as an excuse: habits are hard to give up; doing something repetitively means you can easily do it without thinking. People lie to themselves, that after they decided to give up they 'accidentally' lit a cigarette without thinking about it. The mind is so powerful it can push thoughts you don't want to face so deep that you can do an action entirely subconsciously. This is true. But if a person genuinely lit a cigarette accidentally, without thinking about it, while they were trying to give up, they could just put it out and that would be the end of the matter. They would have no need to blame that accident for the fact that they are back smoking again. That excuse requires a person to believe the lie that the addiction is entirely the drug's fault.

All habits that are hard to give up have the same root causes. It doesn't matter whether it's drugs, gambling, sex, work, telly, nail biting, eating or whatever, it's all about safety. The comfort that is freedom from fear. It is not the repetitive nature of a habit that makes it seem difficult to give up, but its comforting value that makes a person unwilling to let go. The feeling of safety through familiarity creates habits and makes them precious to us, like a child with a comfort blanket or a dummy. In each of us that child part still exists in our brains as stored memories and feelings and each habit and addiction we have is in some way satisfying that need within, comforting that child inside. The familiarity the habits bring comforts the child. When you know you are in a familiar place it seems like home and home represents safety and comfort. It doesn't matter whether the familiar home is a mansion or a hole dug out of a dung heap, it is familiar therefore it is home, - therefore it is comforting. Many things that are familiar feel safe. They may not be safe, but they feel safe. Feeling safe is freedom from fear.

Familiar = Comfort + Safety

Things that are new may create anxiety; things that are familiar generally create comfort. Yet it is also true that something new and different can create excitement and interest and exhilaration; something the same and repetitive can create boredom and depression and a feeling of being stuck in a rut. Both attitudes are true because each attitude is a choice. However, something that is familiar is generally comforting. It doesn't have to be a good thing. It can be a drug or a telly or a difficult relationship with an abusive partner. We cling on to these things because they are familiar and the fear of letting go seems greater than the fear of the consequences of continuing with things the way they are.

The action of lighting a cigarette and holding it and smoking and swallowing are all so familiar there is comfort in all these things. There was no feeling of comfort in the first few cigarettes, because they weren't yet familiar. It is the aspect of familiarity and comfort regarding this habit that we must look at and work through. First, we have to make a decision. Do you really want to continue experiencing this comfort twenty, thirty or forty times a day? There are only two answers.

No, because the price is too high.
No, because the sense of sickness is greater than the comfort.
You feel more sickened than comforted by this action.

Even if your answer is the second answer, the fact is that one of the reasons you have found this habit hard to break is because it is something powerful that touches us in a deep, sub-conscious way. The answer is not denial. That river in Africa will not get us where we want to be. The answer is to recognise, acknowledge and understand that there is comfort in this habit, because it is familiar. Not because the drug nicotine does anything for us, or stimulates feelings of comfort. Not at all. It is comforting because it is familiar and if you don't smoke you will be missing out on that comfort. The thought of missing out on that comfort creates anxiety and fear leading on to panic and adrenaline and we mistake this for withdrawal. If we are missing out on that comfort, then by not smoking we are missing out on something. The decision is, are you willing to miss out on that particular comfort? The problem with this decision is that it is false. It is an

179

illusion. It is a in itself an aspect of addiction, one of the things that keep us addicted. If we make such a decision we are still in the addiction because in reality it is utterly pointless.

I am going to show you that in reality, you are missing out on nothing. How can I say that when I have just proved that smoking is a familiar habit and that familiarity is comforting? Here is the how. All of us have had many comforting habits that, for whatever reason, we no longer have now. Sucking dummies, sucking thumbs, jam sandwiches, biting nails, listening to that song over and over again. Many habits we still have, but some of them, we have let go. Think of a habit you have had that gave you that comforting, safe feeling, which you no longer have. For example you may have had a period of having a particular food regularly, like jam sandwiches or cornflakes. Eventually, after months or even years you just ate something else instead. You moved on and you didn't miss the old jam sandwiches or cornflakes. We call these food fads. Millions of people have food fads. Think of another habit you once had, such as biting your nails or wearing that particular item of clothing well beyond the time it should have been thrown out with the rest of the rags. Once you saw how awful it had become you let it go, you moved on. Having moved on, you have not regretted the passing. You haven't missed those habits, those old sources of comfort. You did not make that pointless decision to do without the comfort it gave you. You simply reached a point where you saw no further point in continuing to do it, perhaps because you didn't enjoy it any more, but, for whatever reason, you simply stopped doing it.

WE DON'T MISS THEM. WE DON'T FEEL DEPRIVED

Millions of people have stopped smoking. We don't miss smoking. In fact we are really glad and proud to feel the freedom and energy we have now. There are some ex-smokers who still have illusions but we have already discussed them. They tend to let everyone know their problems so it can seem that they are in the majority but most ex-smokers are free and we do not miss smoking at all. As far as virtually all habits are concerned, once we are free from them we don't miss them. We don't suffer at the thought of not doing that today. We don't feel deprived.

We see, either through not practising that habit for a while, or before we stop doing it, that the comfort is false. Lots of things are familiar. Lots of things are comforting. This particular comfort has already turned into a nightmare. Being a slave is being a slave. That can be comforting. A comforting habit that has been let go, no longer gives comfort. When you were a toddler you sucked on a dummy and you may have sucked your thumb. You eventually let that go and you don't miss it. So, although it is true that a repetitive habit is comforting it is not true that you miss it after you have let it go.

I have let go. Holding a cigarette or putting it in my mouth is not comforting to me at all. All habits that are given up lose their comforting powers very quickly, smoking especially so because once you are no longer withdrawing you can smell and taste that it is in reality quite obnoxious. You do not miss out on the comfort. Accept this. It is a habit. It is familiar, therefore it is comforting. That's true. You will not miss it. That's true. It is not logical, it is simply true.

Core beliefs

Here we will look at core beliefs and how they can relate to nicotine addiction. By the end of the section you will have greater insight about how core beliefs affect people's lives and how nicotine addiction can be separated from core beliefs so that you can be completely free.

Earlier I mentioned the concept of the inner child. This is a set of thoughts and memories and feelings that are powerful because they were formed when we were very young. They are often called core beliefs. It can be helpful to be aware of this concept, particularly when trying to understand why some of the illusions and beliefs about smoking seem so strong. They can all be broken, but sometimes their power comes from the ignorance of why they are so strong in the first place. We are all shaped by our environment and other people and the messages we receive, especially in early childhood. It is said that your personality and fundamental perceptions and beliefs are formed by the time you are seven. Core beliefs are fundamental beliefs formed early on, in the first few years of life, through which all other thoughts and beliefs have to go through and fit in with. Rather like wearing blue glasses makes the world seem many different shades of blue, even though it isn't really.

Let me give you an example of how core beliefs are formed. Little Harry is four years old. He has an older brother who is two years older than himself. Harry's mother is a 'make do and mend' type of person. Harry's problem is that he is a 'hand me down' kid who wears the clothes his older brother grew out of. Although Harry is too young to really care about such things, there is still an awareness growing deep within his mind that he never has any new clothes and toys. Perhaps he isn't good enough and doesn't deserve them? It's not a thought Harry is capable of putting into words right now, but the sneaking suspicion is there somewhere in the back of his mind. He can't put it into words, but it may come out in other ways. It is his fifth birthday in a couple of weeks and his mum asks him what he wants for his birthday. Harry instantly knows what he wants. He wants a brand new pair of brown leather boots from one of the best high street footwear retailers, the ones who measure your feet with that machine. He doesn't want a toy like other kids, but something new and high quality to wear. Just for assurance that he is worth it and he does deserve it.

His mum, not being one to look a gift horse in the mouth agrees instantly and promptly has Harry measured up and the boots get bought and taken home. Of course, since mum has purchased them and brought them home, Harry naturally wants to put them on and play out in them. There is a problem to this that mum explains. Harry's birthday is one week before bonfire night and she doesn't want the boots ruined so soon, so Harry will have to wait for his birthday to receive his gift. Harry is four years old and doesn't understand a word she has said and a fortnight is another lifetime away on another planet. Naturally there is some tantruming but mum is trying to be the best mum she can be and that means being responsible. There is paddying and tantrums a-plenty during the next few days. The suspicion in Harry's mind that he might not be worth something new and high quality is now tinged with fear that he will never see the boots. Harry's family have a big garden and they have a big bonfire to which the rest of the street comes to share. The morning after bonfire night Harry demands the new leather boots that are his due after a whole week of patience and fear. His mum points out that the bonfire is still smouldering so he will have to wait another day for his new boots. Harry swears he will go nowhere near the bonfire but his mum is a good mum and quite rightly knows better. Harry's fear grows into panic and tantrums ensue. The next day Harry again demands his boots as promised. Mum can still see that the bonfire is still warm and refuses to hand them over. Harry's earlier suspicion, that he is not worth anything new and good, has by now grown into a fully-fledged state of paranoia. The next day Harry tantrums so much that his mum is totally warn down. She has to give him the boots. She quite rightly makes him swear that he will go nowhere near the dirty ashes of the bonfire and if he does he will never get anything new ever again. She ties the laces with much huffing and puffing. Harry is so excited he instantly forgets all promises made and heads straight down into the garden and straight into the middle of the ashes of the bonfire. It has not rained at all since bonfire night and it was a very big bonfire and Harry at that moment discovers a new smell – burning rubber. Of course the boots are a complete write-off, totally ruined, un-saveable.

When Harry realises what has happened he is devastated. The earlier suspicion that he might not be worth and doesn't deserve nice new things is no longer there. Now he knows for a fact that he isn't worth and does not deserve nice new things, he ruins such things. A very strong core belief is formed at that moment backed up by intense feelings. When he goes to face his mother she reinforces his new core belief with the words that he isn't worth nice new things because he ruins them and so he doesn't deserve to have them. These words are accompanied with intense feelings of guilt and shame that Harry already has plus his mother's anger and shame and condemnation. As if this were not enough the core belief is further reinforced with the physical pain of the smacking.

Harry is constantly bemused and frustrated with himself because he is now forty years old and he still seems to ruin every new car he ever has and can never clean his shoes or take proper care of his clothes and he just doesn't have clue why that is.

Once your core beliefs have been established, your mind will try it's utmost to support those beliefs. This will come out in all sorts of behaviours that may have nothing to do with the original thoughts behind the core beliefs when they were first formed. The mind is a powerful thing. So what has this story got to do with stopping smoking? The act of smoking can support a core belief and therefore there is a powerful sub-conscious reason to smoke. Just using this example, if Harry's mind needs to support the belief that he isn't worth and does not deserve anything nice and new then smoking is an ideal way to ruin nice things by burning them and giving them nicotine smells and stains – particularly cars. Self-punishment because of deep shame or beliefs of "I am bad" can also be supported by the act of smoking.

Thus the reasons why you have a great need to smoke may not be apparent and may not be identifiable because they are connected with core beliefs about which you may not have a clue. If you are scratching your head in frustration as to why on earth you are still smoking when you seem to have looked at every other possible reason or issue, it might be that there is something going on in the core belief section of your sub-conscious that you cannot touch. You may not be able to identify that whatever it is that's making you smoke is to do with some core belief issue. Your thought might be that it must just be something in your nature or something genetic or something deep in there you are not meant to know.

So how on earth do you deal with something like that? Let's take a look at the options. You could have a few months of counselling or psychotherapy to get to your core issues and identify the issues that way. That is a valid path to take and it is something I would wholeheartedly encourage. However, you need to be in a particular frame of mind to be doing such a thing for it to work and it may be you are just not in a space that will allow to you to benefit from such a drastic course of action. The other alternative is to just accept it. At the end of the day, if it's to do with your nature or genes, your core beliefs or just the way you are, then that's all there is to it and there's nothing you can do about it.

The reason I have explained what happens in the deepest recesses of the sub-conscious, whether you were already aware about these things or not, is to demonstrate to you that this has not been overlooked as an issue and as a possible reason to continue smoking. Right down to your fundamental core beliefs these issues have been thoroughly investigated. The truth is that it is in no-one's nature or genes or just the way you are or core beliefs to smoke. Addictive and self destructive behaviour may support your core beliefs in some way. So if you have a deep, sub-conscious belief that you don't deserve to be free or clean or strong, then you certainly will support that core belief in lots of different ways. Smoking may have been just one of those ways. It can't have been the only way and it certainly is not the last way. The sudden absence of smoking may feel a little odd at first because of the part it has played in supporting particular core beliefs. Your sub-conscious will very quickly go on to find other ways to support your self destructive core beliefs. It is doing that all the time and it did that for many years before you smoked. Self destructive addictions do support core beliefs but addiction itself only has power at the sub-conscious level. Once a person has become aware of the issues and beliefs surrounding an addiction then they are no longer at a sub-conscious level, they are now at a conscious level. This process separates the addiction itself from the core beliefs.

The bottom line is that this addiction cannot survive or generate uncomfortable feelings simply because it is connected to your sub-conscious core beliefs. You cannot continue smoking for the reason that it is in your nature, your genes or your core beliefs. If you genuinely cannot find whatever it is that is tipping the balance and causing you to continue smoking, all it means is that you need help to find out what illusion it is. Once you find out what your illusion is you will be free.

Fear of success

Now we will take a closer look at possible future fears that could affect your freedom, and how reasons to stop can become reasons to smoke. By the end of the section you will have greater understanding of these concepts and you will be free from the self-imposed conditions that could lead back to smoking.

Before you read the rest of this section you need to complete an exercise. I respectfully remind you at this point that doing these exercises is very important. I urge you to take this seriously and to take as much time and care over this as you can.

Please get a couple of sheets of paper. At the top of one of the sheets of paper write the title,

REASONS FOR STOPPING SMOKING

at the top of the other sheet write the heading,

PROMISES AND AMBITIONS

On the first sheet write down all the reasons you can think of that you have to stop smoking. For example, *"I need to stop because it is making me ill"* or *"It is costing me too much money"* or *"I am sick of it!"* Then write down all the possible reasons you can think of that other people may have for stopping smoking.

When you have completed that, on the other sheet write down all the hopes and dreams and ambitions you have about your life when you are smoke free such as *"I will move forward with my career"* or *"I will feel fitter and healthier and cleaner"*. Also include any promises you may have made to yourself such as *"I will take up squash"* or *"I will go on a world cruise with the money I save"*.

After you have done this, continue reading the rest of this section and keep these lists handy.

One of the possible issues that I had to consider on my path to freedom was the fear of success. I kept failing to stay smoke free and I began to wonder whether there might be some fear of actually succeeding. Now, I can't really see that there is a genuine fear of succeeding, of achieving something I want to achieve, but maybe having succeeded there would be fear about the changes in my life that this success would bring and what this success would lead to. You see I had certain promises to live up to if I succeeded in stopping smoking.

One of those promises was exercise. While I was smoking, every time I went on a get fit trip I would always give up on it fairly quickly because when the going got tough I would reason that there really was no point in trying to get fit when all the time I am defeating the object by smoking. So of course, if I were to stop smoking I would then have no excuse to not do all the very hard work to keep fit. In fact, getting fit was one of my reasons to stop i.e. *"I should stop smoking because then I could get fit"*. As we have already discovered, trying to stop smoking for the reasons to stop is futile, you can only deal with the reasons you do smoke, but I didn't know that at the time. I had tried and failed to get fit many times throughout my life. There was no reason to suppose that I would succeed just because I was not smoking anymore. There are many reasons why I gave up trying to get fit, not just because it seemed pointless being a smoker. There was the reason that I never seemed to have the time and I never seemed to be able to spare the money for the Gym (admittedly if I stopped smoking that would in fact solve that problem), and the reason that I've never been the athletic type anyway and exercise is boring. Other reasons included: this wasn't the right time because there are too many other things demanding my attention, and most people I know get on very well with their lives without a rigorous exercise programme. However, which ever way I looked at it and regardless of the truth, my bottom line was that it was pointless because I smoked. So the consequences of not smoking would be that I would have to fulfil my promise to myself to get fit. The big fear, of course, is that I stop smoking and still fail at the exercise thing. I wouldn't be able to blame it on the smoking this time. I would have to look at other reasons I may not want to entertain, like the possibility that I may be a fundamentally lazy person who didn't have enough self-respect or self-esteem to look after themselves in a healthy way. That thought was very frightening to me.

So as you can see, stopping smoking has its fears. Often these fears are about the promises we make to ourselves about what we are going to do when we stop smoking. There is always the thought in the back of our minds that, despite stopping smoking, we still might fail to do these things, and then it will be our fault, not the fault of the smoking itself. The promises that we make to ourselves are based on the list of reasons we have for stopping smoking.

Another one of my reasons for stopping was that I felt I ought to do more travelling and getting about and visiting people such as relatives and friends. Be a popular person who lived life to the full instead of the sedentary person I was, not wanting to go places where it might be inconvenient to smoke or do things that required more energy than I had. Stopping smoking would mean that I would be free to come and go where and when I please. That I could truly live life to the full. That I would have the energy to do whatever I wanted. So this reason for stopping, though I couldn't see it at the time, represented a tremendous life change. Being someone I had always failed to be. Being that person of my dreams I could never hope to measure up to. What a tremendous amount of pressure that put me under to stop smoking.

Pressure to stop smoking is actually pressure to smoke. They are one and the same thing. We have already discussed this concept in an earlier chapter. The more shame and self-disgust you feel for being a smoker, the greater the need for comfort becomes and the stronger the addiction becomes. On top of this are the promises I have to fulfil if I do stop. I will have to travel to places I don't really want to go, to see people I don't really like just because I have an image of someone who I think I ought to be. It's a lot easier just to not bother stopping smoking at all or at least make yet another attempt, to prove I am trying, but to fail. Failing to stop smoking is an easier prospect than having to live up to my expectations of life as a non-smoker. Failing to stop smoking is an easy failure to live with because it is common and excusable. Failing to live life the way I think I should is a very serious failure indeed, particularly after having so many expectations. So once again, the reasons to stop become the promises made, become the fear of success, become the reasons to continue to smoke.

We have now come across another circle of addiction similar to the adrenaline circle we looked at earlier. The decision to stop is for these reasons, which creates these expectations, which create fear of failing to meet those expectations, which in turn creates a greater need for comfort, which strengthens the addiction and makes it even more difficult to stop.

The way out of this circle of addiction is of course to dump all the reasons you have to stop smoking. These reasons turn into reasons to smoke. The reasons you have to stop smoking are not helpful because they impose conditions. The problem with conditions is that until they are fulfilled they are an excuse to smoke at the first feelings of doubt or anxiety. It is not reasons to stop that you need it is the absence of reasons to smoke. If you have no reason to smoke then you won't smoke.

Now look at the sheets of paper I asked you to fill in at the beginning of this chapter. Look at every item on each list and think about each reason, hope and promise as being a potential source of failure and a way back to smoking. What if you don't achieve these things, what if what you imagine doesn't happen what if those promises are broken. Make a decision with each and every one of the things on both lists that they are nothing to do with smoking or not smoking. Make a decision right now that you don't care one way or another if these things happen or not, they are no longer issues for you. In other words, dump them all. Let each one of them go by making that decision and it being ok. Physically say goodbye to each one in turn.

When you have finished doing that tear up the pieces of paper, then throw them away in a bin. Well done, you are free from them now.

Missing the fight

In the next three sections we will look at the grieving process and possible feelings of depression associated with stopping smoking. By the end of this section you will be able to identify more feelings and the reasons why they are there so that you do not become a victim of mistaken beliefs that are really addiction illusions. Also you will be able to see any feelings of depression in their true light so that they are not linked with the addiction.

I had a relationship with this beautiful girl and it was a relationship of ecstasy and pain. There was constant fighting and arguing, followed by periods of making up and ecstasy. When it ended I found that one of the things I missed was the arguing and fighting, as well as the ecstasy. Would the same thing happen with my fight with nicotine? Would I miss the battle with smoking that had raged in my life for years? Well it turned out I didn't miss that battle. The battle with smoking never actually took up any time or physical action. There was no genuine argument or fighting that took time, action or effort. The fight was all in the head, so there was nothing to actually miss. There was no gap in my life because there had never been anything tangible there in the first place.

I thought I would miss the fight. I thought I would miss trying to sort my life out by stopping smoking. I had become quite obsessed with trying to stop smoking, particularly for the last two years of my smoking. When you become obsessed about something it is difficult to see beyond that. What would I do next? Of course there were the plans to get fit and travel and have lots of friends but what about those empty moments no longer filled with trying to stop smoking or planning yet another way of doing that? What am I going to do with all that time? The bottom line with all these kind of concerns was really about anxiety of moving on. There were things that needed sorting out in my life that had been put on hold for when I stopped smoking. What actually happened when I did stop smoking was that I naturally moved on to those things that had been put on hold and I got on with my life. Such fears had turned out to be fears about nothing. Sometimes we can be afraid and it doesn't have to be about anything in particular. Sometimes we are just feeling anxious of change itself.

Grieving

Whenever changes take place in our lives it usually involves the loss of something. For example, if we change jobs we lose our last job; if we move home we lose our last home, or if we decide to throw out that comfy jumper once and for all, we lose the comfy jumper. Following each and every loss there is a period of grieving. We go through all the grieving stages of disbelief, bargaining, anger, depression and acceptance with each and every loss. Sometimes our loss is so slight we do not grieve, for example the loss of the comfy jumper. There may be some disbelief that it is now gone, that you actually found the courage to throw it away and sometimes you still reach for it now and again. You may bargain that next time you won't let the relationship get to that stage of seriousness and you won't keep a jumper that long again, and maybe if you could find a new jumper that was similar you would treat it better this time and use fabric conditioner every time without fail. Then there's the anger. *Why don't they make them so they last longer - I don't know - everything seems to be made cheap these days not - that my jumper was cheap but I could still be wearing it now if I hadn't caught it on the door handle and made that hole* . . . . .

Then there is acceptance. Now acceptance is a funny thing, it's not the celebration and party after all the other bits of grieving that we think it is. There are no fireworks or cheering crowds or cheery toasts to the lost. Acceptance simply means the absence of any thoughts about the loss one way or the other. Acceptance is emptiness, like a ghost town with the whistling wind and the dry brush rolling past; it is the non-presence of the whole issue in our lives any more.

When you think about stopping, many fears come up about how you will cope with life without smoking. Some of those fears involve the onset of the feelings that come with the process of grieving which, obviously, you are bound to go through after you have stopped. You may have feelings of grief for the smoking itself, or for the feelings you thought smoking gave you; you may grieve the ending of the fight, or the ending of the relationship with the addiction generally. This is certainly a valid fear that clearly merits more grieving than the loss of an old jumper. This type of fear translates as, *"I would be lost without it"*; "what will I do with my hands?"; or "how will I fill the empty spaces". All these thoughts are accompanied by a feeling of anxiety, ready to turn into fear and panic at a moments notice.

Let's look at this process of grieving that you can expect to go through once you are no longer smoking. You may have noticed that I am referring to 'stopping smoking' or 'no longer smoking' as opposed to my usual phrase of 'becoming free'. The reason for

197

this is that the term 'becoming free' is really that place of acceptance after the grieving process has completed. This point is often called 'closure'. So what will the grieving be like and when can you expect to get 'closure'?

Closure, or 'acceptance', is that place where you have no particular feelings about it one way or the other. That doesn't mean you don't have thoughts about the subject, but it does mean that those thoughts no longer trigger any kind of emotional response. The fact of the matter is that so long as you have seen through all the illusions about there being any reason to smoke, or point in smoking; the illusions of pleasure, need or usefulness, then you cannot miss smoking and you can think about it without having any emotional response whatsoever. This happens very quickly and very often immediately. Most people who have worked through this course see no further reason or point in smoking and will therefore experience little or no emotional response to the issue. The reason for this is to do with the grieving process. Grieving can only occur where there is loss. When I stopped smoking I expected to go through some form of grieving process because of past experience, but what I found was that the grieving process didn't happen at all. Maybe it happened very slightly at a sub-conscious level that I didn't notice but I probably didn't notice it because it didn't actually happen. I had seen through the illusions about the need and the pleasure I had previously associated with smoking, just as you are doing now and the upshot was that there was absolutely no sense of loss. I had no illusions that I was missing out on something that helped me in any way or gave me any pleasure therefore there was no sense of loss.

You might think that just the loss of the cigarettes being there, or the actions associated with them: smoking itself, or making sure you have enough to get you through before you have to buy some more etc, would represent a significant loss in your life triggering a sense of loss from which you would naturally grieve. But that didn't happen. Why not? When you take a further look at this the answer becomes clear. Any thoughts or triggers about smoking, cigarettes, ashtrays, packets, lighters, break times etc are not genuine losses. There is nothing tangible going on. You don't have feelings about any of these things when you have seen through the illusions. Just taking the jumper as an example, the loss of the jumper is a tangible loss. The jumper represents warmth and comfort. The grieving isn't really about the jumper, it is about the feelings we associate with the jumper. But with cigarettes haven't you thrown out something that you never really liked in the first place? We don't go through a grieving process about something we never had feelings about in the first place. We can't. We can only grieve for things we are genuinely going to miss, things for or about which we have feelings in the first place. Before working through this course you may have had feelings about smoking – comfort, security or pleasure, but during the course of this course's process you lose those associations and feelings, seeing that they were illusions all along.

So what about the empty spaces? Well again, these are simply illusions. There are no empty spaces. If you used to smoke while going to the toilet, then when you are free you will still be going to the toilet, though perhaps for less time. What do you do with your hands? Well the same thing as you do now with the hand you are not using to hold the cigarette. If you used to smoke while you were watching TV and drinking tea then when you are free you will, I'm sure, continue to have a cup of tea while watching TV. You see, there are no empty spaces. What about break times at work? Most of your friends smoke at this point and now you won't be able to join them. Well, when you are free you can still be with your friends just like the one's who don't smoke now, though if the breaks are in a densely smoke filled room you may not want to spend your break in there. The point is now you have a choice. When you are free you have no need to be afraid of being around smokers. Remember, the physical addiction to nicotine is so slight it doesn't even wake us from our slumber, so a bit of passive smoking can in no way make us addicted again. The only way to become addicted is to fall for the illusions. That is why one cigarette means you are back in the addiction. It is not the cigarette that creates the addiction, it is your mind that created it when you decided you had a reason to smoke. You were addicted before you lit the cigarette. The lighting of the cigarette was simply the final act in securing the addiction in your sub-conscious mind so that you no longer had a choice of conscious will.

The bottom line is simply this: since there is no actual real loss, as you realise when you see the illusions, there can be no grief or sense of emptiness, and missing the fight simply does not happen at all. Those are the simple facts of the matter. There is nothing to fear.

Now please say out loud six times – just do it!

These feelings and this confusion will pass whether I smoke or not.
*These feelings and this confusion **will** pass whether I smoke or not.*

*These feelings and this confusion will **pass** whether I smoke or not.*
*These feelings and this confusion will pass **whether** I smoke or not.*
*These feelings and this confusion will pass whether **I** smoke or not.*
*These feelings and this confusion will pass whether I smoke **or not.***

Depression

If you have ever tried to stop smoking before, you may have experienced a mild form of depression. This depression can feel very powerful at the time, certainly not mild anyway, and all the time you have the idea that smoking a cigarette will lift that depression. You smoke a cigarette and it does lift the depression. What is going on here?

The depression is not because of anything chemical that happens just because you are not smoking. The depression is due to the thoughts you have at a conscious and sub-conscious level. You decide to stop smoking. What have you got to look forward to? A period of going nuts followed by missing out on that pleasure for the rest of your life - and a high likelihood of failure anyway, and all the embarrassment that failure brings, with feelings of being weak in the eyes of others and yourself. Not a lot to look forward to that would inspire a cheerful heart. Not surprising really that you feel depressed. Smoking lets you off the hook, so when you have smoked again the depression instantly lifts. This proves that the depression was entirely due to your negative thoughts and beliefs because there are no antidepressants in a cigarette.

There is another aspect to this feeling of depression that it is useful to note. When you have just given up smoking, when you are tired, the normal tired feeling is mistakenly turned into depression. You feel tired and then you are aware that normally you would deal with this feeling by smoking. The smoking distracted you from the tired feeling. Now that you can't smoke to divert your attention away from your tired feeling you have to wait for something else to distract you from it. Addiction does not know patience; in just a few seconds your tired feeling is turned into feeling absolutely awful, in fact depressed; in fact you are now suffering from depression and if you don't smoke immediately you will have to go to the Doctors for anti-depressants - and how will that look on your medical history? If you don't smoke, not only will you lose your mental health you will also have serious insurance and career problems for the rest of your life and this will lead to poverty and your partner leaving you, leading to more depression, poverty and loneliness. And all because of your refusal to smoke just one cigarette to get over this bit. You can stop again later . . . . ?

Being free from the addiction and seeing through all the illusions is entirely different to the process just described: you feel no depression as a result of being free, you only feel happy, joyous and free. You know why you feel what you feel, you have a process of working through any thoughts and feelings so that you are not a victim, and you now know you will not be missing out on anything for the rest of your life, just gaining instead a tremendous freedom with endless possibilities. Any depression you do feel therefore has got nothing to do with not smoking, so a cigarette cannot lift it for you.

Sleep – Toilet – Smell

This section works through various smaller issues and illusions that contribute to nicotine addiction and keep smokers trapped. By the end of the section you will have worked through these illusions so they cannot lead you back to addiction.

Sleep

Most smokers have had attempts at stopping smoking. Because we are all different, different things are important to us and stopping smoking presents different problems for different people. One of those problems might be that when you have tried to stop in the past you have found it difficult to sleep. Sleep deprivation can be a very serious problem, resulting in tiredness, lethargy and depression. It can interfere with work and relationships and it can be nearly impossible to smile. The fear that stopping smoking may cause sleep deprivation is no small fear for some people. Remember, every fear becomes a reason to smoke unless it is looked at and brought into awareness into our conscious minds. So why does smoking cause difficulties?

Doubt and uncertainty. Doubt and uncertainty cause anxiety which can lead to difficulty in sleeping. Doubt and uncertainty on top of the fear of not sleeping and all the consequences that holds, on top of not actually sleeping can easily lead to more fear which leads to panic and to no chance of sleeping. Which leads to a reason to smoke leading, to a smoke. So let's get to the bottom of this issue.

If you have never or rarely had a sleeping problem then you may think that, perhaps initially, through being a bit excited about not smoking anymore that you may have a couple of late nights. You know full well that this cannot last long so this issue is no big deal to you at all. However, if you have experienced difficulty in sleeping in the past or are currently having sleeping problems then the thought of stopping smoking may well add to your troubles. Alternatively, you may be mistaken in thinking it will solve your troubles. So what are the facts? Well, beyond a very temporary feeling of excitement that may accompany being smoke-free causing perhaps, a couple of late nights, not smoking cannot affect your sleep patterns. Studies have proved that smoking itself is a cause of difficulty with sleeping. Apparently on average a smoker takes fifteen minutes longer than a non-smoker to get to sleep. Being smoke free means there is more chance of getting to sleep, not less.

This is due to physical reactions from the inhalation of toxic fumes, such as increased adrenaline levels, higher blood pressure etc, and also because non-smokers are generally calmer than smokers. A smoker is always having emotional triggers caused by the addiction, whereas a non-smoker's emotions are not continually being altered (unless they have some other addiction). There is another, more subtle problem with the sleep issue for some. It may well be that part of your current sleeping difficulties are to do with how you feel about yourself and smoking may be having a very significant impact on that issue. When you become free it may well solve your sleeping problem either right away or in a little time. Unfortunately, if this is one of your reasons for stopping, then sleeping becomes a condition of your stopping smoking. Once it is a condition, it can then become a concern which can turn into an anxiety, which in turn can lead to fear, panic, not sleeping and back to smoking.

There is only one answer to this. If you were hoping that stopping smoking may help solve your sleep difficulties then be rid of such thoughts. How can you achieve this? Well, remember I suggested you sign an agreement stating that you were not going to make good health a condition of your being smoke-free. You can do the same thing now. Give yourself permission to still have sleeping problems when you are smoke-free. It is ok to see an improvement in those problems as a result of becoming smoke-free, but only if it is also ok for the becoming free to not be the answer to the problem. Even if you have no particular issue with this, you might find that a small, initial difficulty in getting off to sleep can turn into something bigger than it really is. Give yourself permission to have a sleeping difficulty for a while. The more serious the permission you give yourself, the less chance there will be of experiencing the problem. If you do find any difficulty in getting off to sleep, simply lie there with your eyes shut tossing and turning. Providing you are resting your legs and back by laying horizontal and your eyes by shutting them then you will be fine. Your brain doesn't actually need much sleep at all.

Toilet

Every time I tried to quit before, I couldn't go to the toilet. Smoking and toilet went together. Take away the smoking and I got constipated. Should I take laxatives, or change my diet when I stop? I was afraid that having problems like that would get me back smoking. This was fear of failure. In the end I reasoned that the truth is, my body does not need a cigarette to go to the toilet. It wasn't the lack of nicotine, it was simply anxiety making it difficult and the anxiety would pass reasonably quickly. Once I accepted that it was OK to have some difficulty for a time, when it came down to it I found I didn't have any difficulty at all. If I had had some difficulty, it wouldn't have mattered because I had decided it wouldn't. Just like the sleeping problem, once you accept the possible short-term difficulties, they prove not to be difficult. However, there was another problem with the toilet issue – the smell.

Smell

Another change that I had anticipated that relates to toilet, and other things, was that my sense of smell would greatly improve. You'd think that was an advantage, part of the success, being able to smell and taste things better. Fear however, made these things negative. I would smell toilet-y, bodily, nasty smells more. How would I cope with that? Also if my sense of taste got better I would eat more and put weight on. Having an increased sense of smell was a very tiny fear, but it was enough to trigger a mild panic attack. What do I call a panic attack? All of a sudden there is a fairly sharp intake of breath and a wave of heat and prickly sensation that ends up with my face feeling flushed. You may think that this little fear of being able to smell and taste things better, is such a small, unimportant, poxy, pathetic little thing that it just shouldn't matter. But think about this. You only need one reason to light the next cigarette. Once you have a reason to smoke you are already addicted. You can come out of the addiction by the method we have described before: by identifying the physical feelings so that you become separate from them, then finding out what is the thought behind the feelings and what illusion is the thought a result of, and once you see the illusion, you are free again. If you light the cigarette you have lost the opportunity and it may take years (or never) to get free again. Little things are just as powerful as the big things because in the matter of addiction all reasons are equal.

Let's take a closer look at the possible reasons why there can be a real concern/fear about having an improved sense of smell. Whenever a smoker lights a cigarette, whatever smells there were are suddenly neutralised by the over-powering smell of the cigarette smoke. For example, if your Dad has just taken his shoes off after a hard day's work then the answer is to light a cigarette so you overpower the stench with cigarette smoke. Another example would be that there is a smell from the kitchen and you don't want to sort it out right now so you light a cigarette and it covers up the nasty smell from the kitchen. This is bound to lead people on to the mistaken illusion that not smoking increases your sense of smell. If your answer to uncomfortable after-sex smells has been to create smoke then the alternative is to have to put up with the smells and that doesn't seem to be a pleasant prospect to look forward to. This illusion has two aspects. First, it isn't that not smoking increases your sense of smell as such, though it does a bit because obviously you don't have your nose permanently gunged up with tar if you don't smoke, it's that you will no longer have recourse to cover up those unpleasant odours, albeit with a much stronger unpleasant odour that you happen to like because you are a nicotine addict. Second, that those smells you currently are sensitive about seem to be stronger and more unpleasant than they actually are because you are always covering them up with smoke rather than getting used to them. Smoking actually increases your sensitivity to these smells through providing a constant and effective method of avoidance so you never get used to them. Both aspects create the fear that you will smell these unpleasant smells and you won't be able to escape them by creating smoke. What will you do? How will you cope with all these bodily, toilet-y, unpleasant smells all the time?

Instead of allowing yourself to reach the stage of an emotional response, give yourself permission to have an increased sense of smell for a while. A sense of smell is like hearing, it is relative. When there is a lot of noise you can't hear quiet noises, when there is no noise you can hear a pin drop. Smell is the same. If you are in a cowshed with your girlfriend you are far less likely to appreciate her fine perfume than if you are in a nice cosy room alone with her. (Vice-versa with the cologne for the girls by the way!) You may experience being able to smell and taste things better. You certainly hear that from people who are trying to encourage you to stop smoking, but quite frankly, I never noticed it when I stopped. Certainly, even if there is an initial improved sense of taste and smell it won't last because once you are used to it you don't notice it any more. If you work in a cowshed it is not long before you no longer notice the smell.

Bad Breath

There is one smell that smoking seems to cover up effectively – bad breath. Many smokers have two fears about this. Becoming a non-smoker has two risks. The first is that you can no longer cover up the smell of your bad breath and the second is that you can no longer cover up the smell of your partner's bad breath. These fears can be major issues for some people. I'm going to be blunt with you because this is a sensitive issue and I am not a nice person – Smoking does NOT cover up your bad breath, or your partner's. If your breath stinks (as the saying goes, *"There's bad breath and there's bad breath Barney but you could knock a buzzard off a s%!* wagon!"*) then smoking or not smoking will make absolutely no difference. The reason for this is that you can only cover up the source of whatever is causing the bad breath while you are actually smoking. As soon as you stop smoking that bad smell is still there and is still being breathed to the unfortunate world out there. The only solution is to chain smoke.

It is often said that smoking itself creates bad breath. How could it do that? Well, the answer is the tar and the staining. Cigarette smoke leaves deposits on your gums and teeth and these sticky deposits attract food molecules, and after a while of brewing and decaying a terrible pong is created. Not smoking means that your breath probably cause less fainting, not more. When I smoked I sometimes smelt the bad breath of a non-smoker and from this evidence concluded that non-smoker's breath smelled far worse than smoker's breath. I arrived at this nutty conclusion because I was a drug addict dominated by fear. I ignored smokers who had bad breath and focussed on non-smokers who had bad breath and then couldn't remember experiencing bad breath from any smokers. So to my mind it was only non-smokers who had bad breath. Smoking covers up bad breath only for the time you are smoking. It can only cover up your partner's bad breath for the time you are smoking. It does this primarily not by masking the smell but by providing you with some space because if you are smoking you will not be doing this right in front of their face.

Being a non-smoker will mean less chance of bad breath. This does not however answer the fear that you will have to smell your own or your partner's bad breath without being able to cover it up with toxic fumes. The answer to this is the same as the answer to all the other sense of smell problems. Whatever the smell is that you have a concern about, at first you will be a little more sensitive to it until you get used to it and don't notice it any more. Also, just for a while to help make you feel better, you could use mouthwash, maybe even brush your teeth or, dare I say it, visit a dentist. The answer to bad breath is to do these simple things. Using smoking to cover it up, risking disease, amputations, death and financial hardship does seem a tad over the top, using an extremely large hammer to break a very modest nut.

Overeating

The next two sections look at the very important issue of weight.

I will put on weight if I stop smoking.

Let's take a look at this. The first thing that we must establish is that it is NOT certain that you will put on weight. It is however true that many people do put on weight after they have stopped smoking. The second thing we must establish is that those people who do put weight on DO NOT put weight on because stopping smoking causes any kind of change in metabolism; they put weight on purely and simply because they eat more food. The third thing we must establish is that those people who put on weight as a direct result of eating more after stopping smoking almost always lose it again when their eating pattern returns to normal. Eating more after stopping smoking is common because of the anxiety that can accompany anything new and important in a person's life.

This means that you might eat more because you are not smoking. There are several things going on here.

I'll snack as a replacement for smoking.

I'll snack because of feelings of insecurity.

I'll finish every meal and have pudding because I am not rushing to finish to get to that cigarette.

Obesity is just as unhealthy as smoking.

The bottom line is I prefer to be a slim smoker than a fat non-smoker.

Smoking helps you slim.

I'll snack as a substitute

If you snack as a substitute, it means that you believe you are missing out on something. I don't mean that you are consciously thinking, *"I am missing a smoke, so I'll eat something instead."* I mean that somewhere in your head that thought exists, even though you may not be conscious of it. These thought processes are somewhere in there when you find yourself snacking on comfort foods. It may not be that the thought process is actually identifying smoking as being missed, it may just be a feeling that something is missing and it is a similar feeling to hunger, so the answer seems to be to eat something. Unfortunately, it isn't actually hunger. So even when the snack is eaten it does not make the feeling go away, it does not satisfy the hunger. As soon as you stop snacking you are no longer comforted and the emptiness feeling returns.

So how can you handle this so that you are not snacking yourself silly? The first thing to remember is that many people who stop smoking have not yet worked through all the illusions about the addiction, so naturally they are bound to feel that something is missing in their lives. That is why many people eat more when they quit: they are trying to fill a gap or make up for a loss. If you are aware that there is no loss; that smoking never gave you anything in the first place; there was no need to smoke because it didn't help you cope, and it doesn't taste nice, and there is no genuine pleasure, then you cannot feel this sense of loss and you will feel no need to fill any gap. But let's just say for argument's sake that initially after you have become free, the absence of smoking does cause some feeling of emptiness and you find yourself snacking more, then simply be aware that the

212

hunger you are feeling is not for food and the snacking will not fill it. If you are sure and certain about this fact, then after a few times of experiencing this feeling and not snacking on it, it will stop happening. It must stop happening because you sub-conscious has no choice. After a few repetitions of your refusal to attempt to fill a gap that cannot be filled your sub-conscious must accept this, it has no choice, that's just how it works. Once the sub-conscious has accepted this the uncomfortable empty feeling will not re-appear. I am not saying that not snacking on these feelings is easy.

Snacking because of feelings of insecurity

Any change that takes place in our lives is accompanied by feelings of insecurity. This is perfectly natural and to be expected. It would be odd and perhaps a cause for concern if you didn't for a period of time feel some insecurity because your life has undergone a change. But this will pass whether you snack or not. There is a danger here that if you have the thought that you are snacking because of feelings of insecurity, you may come to think that the insecurity was there in the first place and that smoking was comforting that insecurity.

There are two separate issues here. Is there insecurity that isn't just due to the change that has taken place? If there is, did smoking comfort or help you deal with that insecurity? The answer to the first is yes. You are a human being and you have insecurities whether or not you choose to admit or acknowledge them they are certainly there. You had them before you started smoking and you will continue to have them when you are free.

213

In years to come you may deal with some or most of your insecurities or you may deal with none. You may collect some more on the way and deal with them or not. Some of your insecurities are deep and you will have them a long time and some are about an immediate situation. This is where it gets a bit complicated. An immediate situation, such as a small or big change in your life can trigger deeper insecurities that date back to childhood and are nothing to do with what's happening now. This can create anxiety which can trigger adrenaline release which can seem like withdrawal. When you were a child you sucked your dummy or your thumb. Adults can't do that so they smoke or eat or gamble or other things we don't mention. Being aware that this is happening will in itself lessen the impact and you won't be as powerless as you were before you knew what was happening and why.

Deep insecurities from childhood may be firmly entrenched in your sub-conscious mind so you may not know what they are. All you know is that you are suffering a feeling of insecurity and your immediate, habitual thought on the matter is that the problem is that you are not smoking and the solution is to smoke. This of course doesn't work because the same thing will happen the next time. So what do you do with this awful feeling of insecurity that you now know is not due to lack of nicotine? The answer is that it will pass. Whether you smoke or not, it will pass. Whether you snack or not, it will pass. If you are still feeling this insecurity three weeks later then it certainly can't be about the change in your life that is stopping smoking. It must be about something else, in which case smoking cannot solve it anyway and neither can snacking.

I'll finish every meal

The realisation that now you are not smoking you don't have to rush to finish the meal in order to have a smoke might well mean that you finish the meal and even toy with the idea of enjoying pudding because now you have the time to enjoy such things. Add to this the likelihood that initially you will have an improved sense of smell and taste so you might find food and eating more enjoyable than you did before. What you have here is a recipe for a greater intake of food and the subsequent weight that will be put on as a result.

There is a simple and effective remedy for this. You have to develop a new skill. You have to learn to recognise when you are no longer hungry – i.e. when the hunger is satisfied and then stop eating. Now this or course, sounds a lot simpler than it actually is and you may find it much less easy to do than it sounds. So you have to be aware of the reasons why this simple course of action can be difficult. The first reason it is difficult is because it is simply something new. You have probably never done this before, it is a new thing. You have to make a change and all change is, of course, difficult. You could allow yourself some time before you try it by allowing yourself to eat more for a little while, but remember, it is a lot easier to not put weight on in the first place than it is to try and lose it later. So it is much better to develop this new skill straight away.

The other reason it may seem difficult is the same reason we found quitting smoking so difficult up until today. We have certain beliefs that are contrary to what we are trying to achieve. You have been told that you must eat everything on your plate otherwise you are being selfish and ungrateful and are disrespecting the starving children in the Third World. This is one of those absolute laws given to us by the unanimous multitude of parents which we in turn impose on our children without even thinking about it. Please excuse me if you are one of those rare people who have thought about it and don't do it. The upshot of this is that in leaving a plate with a third of the food still on it we are inviting guilt and shame and the loss of the psychological security and comfort that eating gives us. Not a good deal to swap that lovely comfort for all that guilt and shame. When we smoke, the guilt over the starving children doesn't come up because we are too busy suppressing our guilt and shame over being a smoker. Answer – don't put so much food on the plate next time. Unfortunately next time we eat it is someone else who has put all that food on the plate, or we forgot, or that much comes in the packet, or you might as well cook an amount that will definitely satisfy the hunger because you can always leave what you don't want.

I didn't get this course to give up ove-reating, I got this course to quit smoking! It is your choice. You do have a choice. You can choose to do this. After the first half a dozen times that you stop eating when you are no longer hungry it gets really easy to do. It's only the first few times it is difficult because you think you will get hungry a lot sooner after this meal if you leave half of it. Well so what? Genuine hunger is a feeling that is satisfied after a very small amount of food.

Obesity is just as unhealthy as smoking

This thought is a classic addiction trap. Comparing one addiction to another and then deciding to settle for the one you are trying to give up. Is obesity as unhealthy as smoking? Well unfortunately that is an extremely complicated question because it depends on how much and what you are smoking and how much you weigh and how tall you are and what your fat to muscle ratio is? The answer then is no, or yes. The addiction illusions are saying to you that you might as well carry on smoking because if you stop you will get fat and that is worse than smoking in terms of health-risk. This of course is complete nonsense, it is the insanity of addiction and again, you can only have this thought if you think you are giving something up that you like. If you like smoking, then carry on smoking. If you have NOT understood through this course that you don't really like smoking at all, it is just an illusion that is part of the insanity of addiction so you know you are not giving up anything, then you will probably carry on smoking. Linking another addiction to smoking can only serve to con you into continuing to smoke. The question of overeating is a wholly different question. It has nothing to do with smoking. You don't need to smoke for any reason whatsoever, but you have to eat. The two things are entirely separate issues. You can enjoy certain foods because they stimulate your taste buds and this stimulates a good feeling. Smoking stimulates nothing, it does absolutely nothing for you whatsoever, it has nothing to do with eating. The fact that nicotine withdrawal is indistinguishable from the feeling of hunger is the reason why people link the two problems. Because that link exists, people eat more after giving up smoking. Just because the feelings of withdrawal, that feeling of emptiness that results from the sense of loss your brain experiences when the nicotine is washed out, feels like hunger, those people who don't know any different are naturally going to eat more. You do know different. You have awareness. You know that smoking has got nothing to do with eating. You know that some of the hunger you are experiencing is not a hunger for food and eating will not fill that hunger. Because you know all this you simply take charge of the situation and stop eating as soon as you stop feeling hungry. Yes, you will feel hunger sooner so you will eat more meals and snacks and that's fine. To eat a little and often is the most healthy way there is. Eating a little and often will actually higher your metabolism. If you do eat a little more often but much less, then not only will you stop those hunger pangs but you will also lose weight if you need to, due to a higher metabolism. If, on top of this you change what you eat to a healthy balanced diet (whatever that is?), then you will certainly lose even more weight and you will be less likely to suffer from a whole range of illnesses including heart disease and cancer.

You are free to choose to sort out your eating or not but the main point is that it has nothing to do with smoking or not smoking. Separate the two issues because eating right is a large and complex and difficult issue for a great many people, and linking it to smoking is not only wrong, it is part of the subtle trap of addiction that can trick you back into smoking again.

Slim Smoker?

or

Fat Non-smoker?

I'd rather be a slim smoker than a fat non-smoker

For a great many people this is the big one. This is the final reason why many people smoke. It may not be your issue but it is for many people so we need to work through this.

This idea may not be in a conscious sentence like this. It may not be stated as such. It is one of those thoughts that is so far in the back of your mind you can honestly say that is not what you think. If you absolutely know for a fact that this thought does not exist anywhere in your mind because you are already slim enough and you want to be able to put some weight on anyway, then fine. If not, then I want you to find this thought from inside your mind and bring it up into your conscious awareness. Please do that now. Ask the question. *Which would I rather be - a slim smoker or a fat non-smoker?* Seek out the doubt. The obvious answer is that you would rather be a slim non-smoker. But what if you didn't have that option? What if it was either/or? Decide now.

If your genuine and doubtless decision is that you'd rather be a fat non-smoker then clearly you don't have an issue about this or it is so buried you can't find it. Even some people who don't have a particular issue with weight might choose to be a slim smoker rather than the other alternative. Also, many people who don't have a weight problem would still fear putting on any amount of weight so much they would prefer to stay smoking. This is nothing to be ashamed about it's just the way it is for many, many people. It is very common.

The problem we have with this issue is that stopping smoking may mean putting on weight and this is something many people cannot accept. It is the reason why all the good intentions go out of the window at the slightest increase in weight. Smoking and weight have been linked because of the idea that you put on weight when you stop smoking. The rest of the idea, which says you lose that weight naturally as you settle down to living life smoke free gets lost, or is not really believed. A slight doubt about this leads to a bit of anxiety which, at the wrong moment leads to further doubt and fear and panic and a cigarette. Does this mean we have to become willing to be a heavier non-smoker so that any increase in weight does not lead to smoking? No. Certainly not! You do not have to make any such agreement. Any such agreement would, I think, be unrealistic and pointless anyway. No, what we can do with this potential booby trap is to make three other decisions before we actually stop smoking.

1.   *Believe the second half of the idea that any weight gain will be lost naturally.*
2.   *Make a decision to eat healthier (less) so you learn to be slim long term.*
3.   *Completely separate the two issues.*

Your fear may take over and want you to doubt that you lose any weight you might have gained as a result of smoking, so let's separate the fact from the fiction. Is it that one or two people have mentioned they gained weight when they stopped smoking and since then it has spread so that it now forms an illusion that is part of the addiction? Or has this issue been studied and found to be definitely false? Well fortunately I do have the answer to this one. It has been studied by the medical profession and it has been established that most people (not all) do put on weight after stopping smoking and they subsequently lose that weight and get back to their regular eating patterns. This is a scientifically proven medical fact. There is no theory we can ridicule, it is straightforward statistics. If you put weight on you also lose it. Simple as that, it is fact. So you can now for definite go right ahead and believe that if you put on any weight after stopping smoking you will lose it quite naturally later. No problem.

However, what if still feel some doubt and anxiety that you may end up being heavier permanently. You might be one of those unusual people who don't get back into a regular eating pattern and lose weight naturally. You might just end up a little bit heavier long term as a direct result of stopping smoking. This is great! What a fortunate and lucky happenstance! It means that you then are presented with an opportunity to learn to eat healthily and you will have the perfect excuse and motivation to do so.

Maybe there is some doubt about what I have just said. Your doubt can only come from the difficulty you have already about the weight issue. You may already feel quite defeated by it and stopping smoking and risking more weight may be just too much for you. Here is the good news. Becoming free from your nicotine addiction will also enable you to get free from your food addiction. You can use the same process of looking at what you believe: what do you feel, what are the illusions with regard to eating?

Yet more good news is that because you have successfully freed yourself from a killer addiction you can carry that success forward and use it to give you the confidence to tackle other issues. You can beat this one, you can beat the next one.

More good news is that you are showing your sub-conscious and your child inside that you are choosing what's best for you and you are making the effort to love and respect yourself. A person who demonstrably shows that they love and respect themselves is a person who will solve their issues. Becoming free from the nicotine addiction shows you are a person who is willing to make great effort to love and respect themselves. This certainly impresses your sub-conscious mind, and you will find it easier and preferable to tackle other self-defeating behaviours as a result. People who have got free from nicotine addiction very often do tackle other issues and they end up losing a lot of weight and getting fit and running marathons. This is very common. What you are doing right now is simply the beginning of a very different life of psychological and emotional growth if you choose it. It is all up to you, the world is your oyster. You can do whatever you want. Certainly a little weight gain is a no more of a problem compared to the problem you are facing right now - your nicotine addiction.

There is one final point we need to be aware of. No matter how aware you are that any weight you put on will be lost naturally, and no matter how determined and resolute you are to be willing to tackle any other self-defeating behaviours, there is one subtle trap that will get you back smoking. It is a serious addiction illusion that you need to take seriously so you are not its next victim. It is the link. The link between smoking and weight. In reality **there is no such link**. Smoking is smoking and eating is eating and they are completely separate activities. The one similarity, the hunger feeling, does have its effect and does cause a little more eating than usual, so weight is gained by many people. This tenuous chain of causes has given birth to a link between smoking and weight. The only way forward through this is to separate the two in your own mind.

Slim Smoker? or Failed non-smoker?

If you want to smoke, smoke; if you don't then stop. If you want to eat too much, eat too much; if you don't then eat less. They are completely separate issues because stopping smoking can only cause temporary weight gain that will be lost anyway. If the weight gain isn't lost then you have a problem with eating not smoking! If you already have a problem with weight then stopping smoking may help you with that long term but it has nothing to do with your weight problem in itself. Your smoking and your weight issues have similarities but they are separate. **There is no link!**

Smoking helps you slim

People who stop smoking feel a hunger which they try and fill with food, so they put on weight. If you don't understand this, it translates into smoking helps you slim because not smoking means you put on weight. This does not apply to a non-addict. It can only apply to an addict. The thought is completely wrong even for an addict, because as we have discussed already, just about everyone who has ever stopped smoking and then put some weight on has lost that weight after a while because they settle down to the regular eating pattern they had when they smoked. Also, if a slightly over-weight non-smoker starts smoking, they do not lose one ounce of weight. Smoking does not help anyone slim or stay slim or avoid putting on weight. Smoking and weight are completely separate issues. You personally may have a problem with both issues, but until you separate them from each other, both issues will continue to defeat you.

What if the reason you smoke is to control your weight and it is working for you? You smoke for this reason and as a result, your weight is controlled. The answer, unfortunately, may be too simple for you to accept. The answer is that you are completely and utterly wrong. You are trapped in a classic addiction illusion. Many women heroin addicts believe the same thing about heroin – and nicotine. It is part of the terrible insanity of addiction. I am not trying to insult your intelligence. I myself was trapped in various drug and behavioural addictions for decades, and I have a university degree! It's not about intelligence. Having mistaken beliefs is not about there being something wrong with you. We have all been wrong. Some of us, like me, have been terribly wrong about some things for decades. It's part of having the whole human experience thing. If you think that smoking controls your weight – yes, even if you have proof - you are simply in one of those classic addiction traps and your thoughts are insane, wrong, incorrect, misguided, misinformed, sadly mistaken, in error, not right, not correct, unrealistic, living under a gross misconception, self-deceived, misled, ill-informed and deluded.

It is the link that is the trap. The link in your mind. You can't risk stopping smoking because of the weight you think you will put on, and you can't control your weight because, instead of learning how to, you just carry on smoking, expecting that to control your weight - which incidentally it isn't. You're not going to learn to eat healthily while you smoke because you believe the smoking is controlling your weight for you. You're not going to stop smoking because you will put on weight. You are completely stuck in this situation because smoking and eating are linked in your mind. Detach these issues from each other and you will have the choice to solve both. Detach them now.

Weight – My Story

I'm going to share with you my own story in regard to the weight issue. I am doing this firstly, so you can identify with my thoughts and feelings about it, even though my initial thoughts and feelings about this issue may have been wildly different from yours. We are different people, so not everything in my story is going to be the same as yours, but hopefully you will be able to identify with enough of it in order find it helpful to you. Secondly, because my journey through this issue will hopefully provide you with some hope or inspiration or at least enable you to form your own possible map to work your way through this issue yourself.

Firstly I will tell you about my situation when I was smoking with regard to the weight issue, then I will tell you what happened when I became free and finally I will share with you what is happening today.

How it was

From being a child and throughout my life I was always very thin, or at least, I thought I was very thin. I was certainly on the slim side but I always thought I was just too skinny and puny. I never had a big appetite and I never finished meals. If I had a takeaway I could never finish it and there would be usually at least a third, if not half the food left on the plate by the time I'd had enough. I used to buy weight gain supplements that you get from body building type shops, but because I found them so filling I didn't eat the meal I would have had if I hadn't drunk the weight gain drink. I tried weight lifting to build some muscle but it never lasted because I was always dreadfully unfit and I smoked like a chimney, so any exercise really wore me down and I was always quickly disheartened and gave up. I tried eating the sort of foods you are always warned against eating but I could never eat anywhere near enough to do anything but maintain my extremely light weight. I kept promising myself that one day I would stop smoking and then I would be able to exercise and build muscles and I would also find my appetite because you put weight on when you stop smoking or at least, that's what I'd heard.

Then I received some bad news. I was waiting in a doctor's surgery one day when I saw this leaflet on stopping smoking. I picked it up and read it while I was waiting. The leaflet said that they had studied the effects of stopping smoking and one of their findings was that most people put on weight after stopping smoking but they just about always lose it again when their eating patterns return to normal. I was devastated. All of a sudden one of my main reasons for stopping smoking had been taken from me. Even though I might gain some weight after I stopped smoking I would most likely lose it again later. Knowing me I probably wouldn't put any on in the first place anyway.

Because one of my main reasons for stopping smoking was now gone, when I was working through my issues about smoking, like you are doing now by working through this course, I had to come to some sort of deal with myself. I had to make an agreement with myself that even though I probably won't put weight on when I stop smoking and even if I do I will probably lose it again, that was OK and I would stop smoking anyway. I recognised a possible issue that could arise after I stopped smoking and sorted it out straight away rather than let it creep up on me later at a moment of doubt and uncertainty. I could have ignored the issue and risked feeling bitter that I hadn't put on weight when I stopped smoking. Then I could have had the thought of "what's the point" and started smoking again. But instead of risking that, I came to an agreement with myself beforehand.

What happened

Then I went on to work through all my issues and become free from nicotine addiction. After which, I found that I was enjoying my food more than I had ever done and I wasn't rushing to finish my meal to get to that next cigarette. I also encouraged myself to try lots of sweets and puddings that I would never have gone near when I was smoking. You must remember, I wanted to put weight on, there was no concern on my part whatsoever about being overweight, that was something I couldn't imagine at that time. Well, a year on and two trouser sizes bigger later I had put a decent amount of weight on. Everybody who knew me said that I looked much better because of the added weight and I felt really good about it. I no longer felt weak and puny and my confidence grew. However, this was not to last. Around about the point of reaching the next trouser size up I began to have doubts about this new weight. I was beginning to feel that it could get out of control and though others said I looked good, I could only agree with that assessment if I had my clothes on. I was seriously beginning to not like what I saw with my clothes off.

At this point realisation that things were getting out of hand another disturbing development arose. When I got up from my bed or from sitting down for any length of time, my knees and angles were complaining. They were finding it difficult to carry this new weight and they were aching. I found it was taking me quite a while to walk properly if I had been sleeping or sitting for a long time. I did not like this at all; I was beyond the limit of weight that I was comfortable with. Also, at this time someone close to me who had always carried a little too much weight had a heart attack, and that freaked me out as well. It made me look at myself and my own weight and my eating habits in general. Then something happened that really surprised me. When I tried to cut down on the amount I ate and to stop eating certain foods that were particularly fattening I found that I couldn't.

I had never considered the possibility of such a thing happening to me. I was shocked and somewhat disturbed. Now, I must point out that I wasn't actually overweight. I was at the top limit considered healthy for someone of my height. So when I expressed my concerns to other people they looked at me with a certain amount of disbelief because to them I just looked normal and though I was looking a little on the chubby side I certainly didn't look like I had any kind of weight problem as such. But despite this, I had cause to worry because I was just getting heavier and I was having great difficulty stopping getting heavier, let alone thinking about getting lighter and I didn't like it. It was about this time that the idea flashed into my mind that I could start smoking again.

I thought that if I started smoking again I would eat less at each meal and where today I might have a packet of crisps or some tea and biscuits I would simply have a smoke instead. There were a couple of problems to this idea. Firstly, cigarettes really do taste foul and I knew I would have to get myself addicted before I could start enjoying them again. Secondly, I was simply swapping one unhealthy habit of eating too much for another killer habit of nicotine addiction with all the slavery and low self-esteem and inconvenience that comes with it. I could see that this was a rather drastic and stupid solution to the problem. The other risk with starting smoking again was that although I had heard that smoking helps you slim and I could see how it could help you slim I didn't actually know whether this was true or not. I had no actual evidence that this was anything other than yet another myth, another addiction illusion. I might continue to eat just as much and continue to put on weight as well as smoke.

Food addiction?

There was another possibility that I had not yet considered. I had learned how to become free from my nicotine addiction so maybe I could learn to become free from my food addiction. This account of what happened to me, by the way, is told here with the benefit of hindsight; it was not as ordered and calm and logical at the time I assure you. I had to ask myself the question, *"Is this really an addiction? Could this be truly classed as an addiction - because after all I'm not actually obese?"* So I began to think about what an addiction really is. It is very to find a specific medical definition because there are more than one and they keep changing, so I had to decide for myself about what an addiction is. I decided that an addiction is something I do very regularly; it is something that is bad for me in some way, and it is something I can't stop myself from doing even though I want to. This became my definition of addiction. The next difficulty with calling this particular problem an addiction was that it is different from drug addiction because you don't need drugs but you do need food. You can stop taking drugs and you can stop gambling and you can stop chewing your nails, but you can't actually stop eating, so surely therefore you cannot view this problem as an addiction.

Then I realised that it was the specific word for the addiction that needed identifying. Through dealing with all the illusions and word games in my head that related to all my other drug addictions, including nicotine, I realised that you sometimes have to really get into these thoughts and illusions to see what they are about. Sometimes the key to doing this is to simply find the right word. Instead of calling this a food addiction I could call it a snack addiction because I no more needed to snack than I needed to smoke, drink or shoot heroin. That was fine but it didn't cover official meal times, where I could put loads on the plate, eat it all and have pudding afterwards. I could still overeat even if I didn't snack. Then I saw that I had found the right word. It was the word 'overeating'. It was overeating that was my problem. Overeating was the addiction. I am not addicted to food I am addicted to overeating. The word overeating means that I eat more food than I need, to the point of it being unhealthy and potentially damaging and dangerous. Just like smoking, it was affecting my self-esteem by causing me to have

232

an appearance that I was unhappy with. I eat food because I need to because I am hungry, I overeat not because I need to, not because I am hungry but because . . . ?

Metabolism

I realised that I needed to do just the same as I did with my smoking addiction and find the reasons why I was doing it. I looked closely at my thoughts. One thought was that it wasn't just the fact that I had stopped smoking that had caused my weight gain. It was also because I had hit a certain age when your metabolism changes. Everybody who gets to my age has a lower metabolism so you don't need to eat much before you put on weight. There were a couple of problems with this thought. One was that, regardless of a change in my metabolism, it was indeed an indisputable fact that after stopping smoking I chose to eat like a pig. The other problem was that I had read an article in a magazine years ago. This article was about a study scientists had conducted in order to discover differences in people's metabolic rate and how that affected their weight. One of the experiments was to put people of different weights and ages into a controlled environment for a number of weeks. In this environment they completely controlled all the food the people were allowed to eat and each person had to eat all the food they were given. They found that people of similar ages had the same metabolic rate. It didn't matter how much they weighed before the experiment, by the end of the experiment they all weighed pretty much the same. They did find differences in metabolic rate with different sexes and different ages, but they also found that these differences were very small in terms of how much weight people ended up with. So what you eat and how much you eat determines your weight, not your metabolic rate. It is very hard indeed for some people to believe that it is the amount of food that you eat and not your metabolic rate that determines how heavy you are. I don't particularly want to get involved in this dispute. However you are seeking answers and it is my responsibility to give you those answers.

Part of the answer is that, maybe it is possible in a few rare cases, being overweight it is due to a persons metabolic rate rather than the amount they eat. It may be that for a few rare people they put on weight just by eating the same as your average slim person. I don't believe it myself and I will tell you why.

There is evidence to support the fact that it is how much we eat and not the metabolic rate. There is no evidence to the contrary – except people's personal experiences. The problem with people's personal experience is that we all live to a certain extent in our various illusions. Our maps of reality are not always reliable. Drug addicts lie about their drug use, smokers lie about how much and the reasons why they smoke and over-eaters lie about how much they eat. These are not dishonest people. There are people living in their illusions. For example someone can say they haven't eaten all day because they are on a diet yet they may have drank a litre of pop and in reality consumed thousands of calories their bodies didn't need. The drink didn't even satisfy any hunger at all. The answer to this is the same as the answer to nicotine addiction. The truth will set you free. Look for where you are wrong. If you look you will eventually find. Stick to being right and you will stay where you are. Keep the same thoughts, keep doing the same things and the results will probably end up the same.

Now please say out loud six times – just do it!

These feelings and this confusion will pass whether I smoke or not.
*These feelings and this confusion **will** pass whether I smoke or not.*
*These feelings and this confusion will **pass** whether I smoke or not.*
*These feelings and this confusion will pass **whether** I smoke or not.*
*These feelings and this confusion will pass whether **I** smoke or not.*
*These feelings and this confusion will pass whether I smoke **or not**.*

Self-esteem

The next issue I looked at was my fear of becoming thin and puny again. When I looked into my thoughts a little deeper I discovered that being thin or heavy was all about how I looked and that how I looked was connected to my self-esteem. At this point in my life I had done a lot of work with internal messages and self-esteem so this area was familiar to me. My self-esteem was wrapped up in what others thought of me rather than what I thought of me, so me looking my best was disproportionately important to me. It was out of perspective and it was an unhealthy motive. When what others think about me becomes more important to me than what I think about me, then I am putting how I feel about me into someone else's hands. Others then control how I feel, not me. It had made me feel really good about myself when other people had complimented me on how well I looked with the extra weight, but when others started to say negative things like, *"that's a bit of gut you've got there"* I was really upset and concerned.

I decided I needed to put what I think of me at the top of the list. I thought, and my body was giving me the message, that on the whole my life would be better if I was lighter and thinner and fitter. Another part of me that always loves me unconditionally and never judges at all, thought that me learning to love and respect my body was a choice I could definitely make. It also suggested that at the same time I could choose to love and respect my body and myself as I am right now. I found that very difficult but I chose it anyway. So how do you love and respect your body? I didn't know how to do that because I had never done it before and no-one had ever taught me that it needed doing, let alone how to do it.

Taking responsibility

One of the first things I did was take responsibility. This came about quite accidentally. I was trying to think of a way to accept me and my body as I am today. I came across a self-esteem tape on which it was suggested that you go to a mirror and apologise for any bad thoughts you have about your body. You had to strip naked in front of a full length mirror and apologise to all your bodily parts for saying things negative and having thoughts about them not being good enough for you. The reasoning behind this is important to know so I will explain it. Most people do not like their own bodies. This is because the ideal weight and shape that films and advertising tell us is acceptable takes hours of workout per day and a strict organised diet, none of which most people have time for. Most people's bodies do not come up to the advertising people's idea of ideal, so most people feel shame for their bodies' appearance even when there is no weight problem. Most people consider themselves too fat or too thin or not muscular enough or too hairy or too short or tall etc. Even those people who pose and model for the advertising people in the first place have these doubts and feelings of not being quite good enough. That's why many models develop eating disorders such a bulimia and anorexia and the blokes get hooked on gym and steroids. They just can't accept the way they look and it is these people who in our eyes look the best. Is this a crazy world or am I? Probably.

So there I am stark naked in front of this mirror apologising to my body. No, it's me. I'm definitely crazy. While I'm doing this I realise that there is another sub-conscious issue coming up into my conscious mind. It is the issue of blame. I discovered at this point that I have been blaming my body for not being good enough. I have been blaming the body I was issued with at birth. It was the fault of my genes and my metabolism and nothing to do with the garbage I sling down my throat on a daily basis or the TV I watch for endless hours instead of the exercising that would do my body good if I cared enough about myself to do it in the first place. I had been blaming a part of me that had no choice in the matter at all, my body. I realised that I had to take responsibility for this issue and stop blaming my body, my genes, my metabolism, the canteen at work, the supermarkets and the food manufacturers. It was my responsibility to inspect, look at and assess the stuff I gave my body to deal with and sort and use. It was no-one else's responsibility but my own.

Do I have the time to prepare healthy foods to take to work instead of buying the rubbish they sell? Do I have time to find the right diet and exercise plan? Do I even know what's good for me and what isn't? Do I have time to find out and reach out for help because I don't know how to do this? These are all choices not proper questions. There are many things I do, like watching TV or reading etc that I don't need to do and I could use that time to do those things I am wondering if I have time for. So I set about trying to find out what is healthy eating and what level of exercise I could do. Once I began to look in libraries and on the internet I was deluged with information about all kinds of diets and exercise plans and theories. I knew enough to avoid the nutty schemes - *buying this course of pills will solve your problem for you without you having to actually do anything.* From all this information it became apparent that the healthiest way forward was to stop eating when I am no longer hungry. Eat a little and often rather than fewer and larger meals. Eat less carbohydrates like pasta, potatoes, rice, chapattis and sugar. Exercise three times a week with something that is consistent such as swimming, exercise bike, jogging or rowing. I chose swimming. The benefit of all this was not just weight control, it was also about having more energy, feeling good about you because you cared enough and made the effort for yourself. There were also other benefits such as being more protected against bugs and viruses and heart disease and cancer.

There is a song, *"Keep young and beautiful if you want to be loved."* There is another song that I made up all by myself, *"Love yourself first and foremost if you want to make the effort to look after yourself so that you look young and beautiful, and then being loved by others will not be so important to you any more."* It's not that easy to remember and it doesn't fit with the tune, but I like it.

How it is today

This is just my journey. You may well feel that none of this has any relevance to you and you are listening to a complete nutter. That's fine. All I can really do is share what has come up for me in the hope that this might help you to find your answers. I am still trying to change my life in terms of eating and exercise because this is a constant concern and requires sticking to and making the effort. It is a choice I have made for myself and I reap the benefits when I do it and I suffer the consequences when I don't. I also try my best to accept the fact that sometimes it seems like one pace forward and two paces back, and I'll let you know when I become a saint but it hasn't happened yet – thought of course I am getting very close.

The fundamental point is, smoking and weight problems are separate issues. While ever you link these two issues together it's extremely unlikely, maybe even impossible, that you will solve either issue. You may have a weight problem, you may not. If you do have a weight problem now, stopping smoking will not take away that weight problem for you, you'll still have a weight problem and you will have to deal with that separately. If smoking is the problem then you have to deal with that problem, it's got nothing to do with your weight problem. So if you have a smoking problem and a weight problem then you can either deal with your weight problem before you deal with the smoking problem, or you can deal with your weight problem after you've dealt with the smoking problem. You could even try to solve them both at the same time. So you could admit straight away that you have an overeating addiction and deal with that at the same time as your nicotine addiction. You do have these choices. You can choose to solve them one at a time or both at the same time, either choice is valid, either choice is good. You can use the same techniques as the ones you are learning to become free from the nicotine addiction, i.e. look at the feelings, thoughts and the illusions and at what the truth really is, because it is the truth that will set you free.

All the answers that you need can be found if you look for them. All the answers that you need are already in you, they are within your own self, you already have them. But what we need is a way to get to them and the way to get to them is to reach out for help. Reaching out for help will enable you to find the answers you already have within you. Like today, you have a smoking addiction and you are reaching out for help by working through this course. I'm sure you have already realised that I am teaching you nothing, I am simply helping you to find the answers that are already inside you, the answers that you already know. You can also choose to do this with any eating problem, with any weight problem. That's what I did. I went out and got some books and I looked on the internet and I found answers confirming what I already really knew. The rest of it was just my willingness to love and respect myself and to make that effort for me in the same way that I would make an effort for anyone else I loved. I had to then make that effort for myself which I find difficult; I find it a lot easier to love and make effort for someone else. Today, I am trying to change that so that I can learn to love me and to make the effort for me. Make the effort to go swimming, make the effort to book that game of squash with so-and-so and make all those arrangements, make the effort to do those exercises. Sometimes I do other things to help with this goal such as meditations and affirmations. I make the effort to be selective in what I eat, what I put in my body, make the effort to care enough to keep on recognising when I'm no longer hungry and I no longer need to eat the rest of the stuff that's on the plate and, that's the easiest thing of all. It's also just about the most important answer of all. I can do it today and you can do it today too. You really can. I know you can and you know you can, so choose it if you want.

Why it is easy

In this section we will look at positive and negative attitudes regarding stopping smoking. By the end of the section you will be able to choose positive thoughts and ideas so that you can be free.

The list

When we make the decision to get free from nicotine addiction, our mind automatically comes up with a huge list of the reasons why it is going to be difficult, if not impossible to do so. It produces, from what seems to be a ready made list hidden round the back, a list of reasons why it is difficult, plus all the fears, illusion and feelings that are coming your way to do with the addiction. The biggest fear, of course, being the fear of failure. This first list that your mind comes up with as soon as you make the decision to stop, is an instant mountain that seems impossible to climb. This mountain; this list of reasons why it's difficult; this list of fears; this list of on-coming uncomfortable feelings, is addiction. That's what addiction really is. It's got nothing to do with the drug. Addiction is essentially this list or reasons why it is difficult or impossible: it is this list of fearful feelings.

This list of thoughts that your mind produces (as soon as you make the decision to stop) produces feelings. The feelings that these thoughts produce are initially feelings of anxiety. This first feeling of anxiety is not so big at first. We can still over-ride this feeling with our conscious mind and continue through. The anxiety then triggers more thoughts and feelings as to why it is difficult or impossible to break free. This induces a little more anxiety. By this time, the anxiety you are feeling is causing some concern in your sub-conscious mind, and your sub-conscious mind translates this as there being some kind of threat, some danger coming up in the immediate future. Your sub-conscious mind, if it's working correctly, will then stimulate the production of adrenaline. When that tiny amount of adrenaline is introduced into your system your heart beats faster, your muscles are generally stimulated, your blood pressure rises and your breathing quickens.

God calls this good body design, good survival design. An addict calls it withdrawals. As soon as the addict notices these physical symptoms, because the addict is blaming the drug instead of what's actually happening - that there is adrenaline in the system - then of course the blame is put on the decision to stop. So now we don't just have a list of reasons as to why it's difficult, we also have what an addict would call physical withdrawals. This can be very worrying and very frightening because it can get very uncomfortable, so the anxiety is now turned into very serious fear. The sub conscious mind translates this into definite and immediate danger of something really harmful happening, so it then quite rightly stimulates an even bigger dose of adrenaline in your system. By this time, of course, the addict, not recognising that their mind and body are working perfectly for their survival, simply recognises it as yet more terrible withdrawals. This feels really bad and the addiction is blamed for it all. Instead of just uncomfortable feelings and fear, there is now sheer and utter panic and terror. It is at this point that an addict becomes willing to single handedly invade Antarctica barefoot over broken glass to get his or her fix.

We are going to look at all the reasons why it is easy to become free from nicotine addiction and why it is easy to stay completely free from this addiction permanently. To this end we are going to draw up an alternative list to the *'list of reasons why it's difficult'* that causes what we call withdrawal. We are going to look at why it is easy to not smoke.

Easy list

I find it very easy to not smoke because I am not withdrawing from the last cigarette I smoked. That was a long time ago and there is no nicotine at all in my system so there is no withdrawal. Addiction, however, is not really much to do with the actual chemical withdrawal; addiction is mostly about fear, and fear mostly stems from ignorance. Having gained such a deep, full and extensive awareness of what is happening physically, mentally and emotionally is clearly going to lessen the fear to the point at which, if you are not feeling any fear, you are not suffering any withdrawals, because, at the end of the day, withdrawals are all about fear and the adrenaline that comes with fear.

It is easy because when you get up on a morning and go about your day to day business you just don't think about it, it's not an issue any more, there's no debate going on in your mind. Initially, it's all about the debate inside your head: *"well I'd like to smoke because"*, or *"I need to smoke because I need to cope with this or that"*, or because *"it's a pleasure and I miss that pleasure"*. When

244

you no longer have this debate; when you've made the decision that you don't actually need to smoke to cope with anything at all ever; when you know for a fact that the only pleasure you ever had from smoking was an illusion and in reality you never had any genuine pleasure; when you know that you cannot experience any relief from the withdrawal you are not having: **then** there is no debate left in your mind, you are not arguing with yourself about whether to smoke or not, and **as a consequence of having no debate, there are no feelings about the issue one way or another.**

The Process

To return to what we've discussed earlier about the process that takes place in your mind regarding the feelings, first, there is a thought and then there is a feeling. The thought may not be conscious; it may be sub-conscious (i.e. you are not aware of the thought itself, only the feeling), but whether you are aware of the thought or not, there are no feelings without thoughts, there is always a thought first. Obviously, if there is no debate going on in your mind as to whether to have a smoke or not; whether there is any pleasure in it; whether you could do with one to cope with this, that or the other; if none of that exists in your mind because the debate has been sorted out and you've made your decisions, then you cannot have a feeling about the issue one way or the other. You cannot suffer from withdrawals, you cannot suffer from the occasional twinge about it, and you can't suffer from any of the panic attacks that you may have experienced before if you've ever stopped before. If you've ever had any length of time when you've stopped smoking, you may or may not have experienced feelings about it at first, but there would have come a time when you did, when you had a thought that suggested that a smoke would be to your advantage, and that thought induced a feeling. If you tried to counter that thought by saying no, I don't need one, the feeling induced would be one of panic. This would lead you back into the same old debate, and all in all, it would probably seem easier to have a smoke. Not that it would be easier, it just seems that way: that's part of the illusion of addiction. Sometimes it will tell you that it is easier to smoke than it is to stay smoke free.

A ridiculous thought! How can it possibly be easier to poison yourself than not to? It is utterly ridiculous, but it is a thought that ex-smokers have and that's what starts them smoking again. When you definitely know that the thought that says it is easier to have a smoke at this point than to resist smoking is ridiculous, you just don't think it. Think of another ridiculous thought. You might see a car and the car is silver. You don't then go on think *"oh no, it's a green car, let's have a debate about this.* You can clearly see it's silver and it would be absolutely ridiculous to debate as to whether it might be green. It's the same with smoking. Any thoughts you might have that it's easier to smoke than to not smoke are ridiculous thoughts. How can it possibly be easier to spend that money to burn those leaves, to inhale those toxic fumes? It's a ridiculous thought and when you know that, it's the end of the debate. There is no more debate, there are no more thoughts about the issue, so there are no more feelings kicking off. It's acceptance, the absence of thoughts, feelings and problems about that issue. The total ending of this debate. It doesn't require will-power, it doesn't require any effort on your part. Effort is only required when you are making decisions about what is true and what isn't; what is sane and what isn't; what is ridiculous and what isn't, and what are the lies and illusions that make up addiction. Once you know all these things there is no debate and it is easy. We have been through all these things in this course though you may have to go over some things yourself later and maybe figure one or two things out on your own. But at the end of the day, the process you have been given in this course is about being able to work through these thoughts and feelings so you are no longer the victim of them.

You have a twinge or you have a bit of a panic. You realise that this is a feeling, you identify the physical symptoms so you detach yourself from it. When you've identified the physical symptoms, then you can have a look at the thought behind them. What kicked off? What happened? What did you see, did someone say something? When you have identified the thought, you can look at the thought itself. Is this a valid thought, is there something we need to deal with here, what specifically was the thought? Maybe it went something like, *"well I've got a three hour meeting ahead of me during which I cannot smoke and usually when I've been facing this situation I've smoked two or three cigarettes in a row to top up on nicotine to get me through. Because I'm not smoking two or three cigarettes, the fear that comes with that thought kicked in and that's why I had these feelings"*. As soon as you become aware of what just happened, of what thought created your feelings, you'll find you are no longer feeling those feelings anyway. Even if they linger you can realise that there is probably still some adrenaline in your system from the initial thoughts and feelings and it can take a little time to clear. That's all it is. It will pass, and it will pass very quickly. It will pass as soon as you stop thinking about the debate. It's no good trying not to think about it: you just carry on doing whatever it is you are doing with your life, having made the decision that it was a ridiculous idea that created those feelings; those feelings are going to pass all by themselves whether you smoke or not, and you just get on with your life.

Do you know, that happens very rarely once you choose freedom and it really does stop happening altogether. It completely stops, you don't get twinges, you don't have these thoughts coming up, and you don't have this debate. By the end of your working through this course you may find you don't experience any of these thoughts and feelings at all, and even if you do, they pass so quickly because you no longer have the fear that you had before. You've got so much more awareness, you're not full of illusion and ignorance and fear. You are full of knowledge and awareness and power, and you no longer need to be afraid of any feelings that come up because you have a process to work them through with.

Working through any thoughts and feelings that arise from time to time in the initial stages is a natural and inevitable process. Obviously for the first few days after your last cigarette you are bound to be obsessed with this issue, but it will pass and believe me, when it goes, it goes. The issue just disappears. Staying smoke free is so easy. In fact, to describe it as being easy is actually misleading, as you can only say that something is easy if you actually have to do something. It's like saying that as an ex-bricklayer I find it easy to not build a brick wall. I don't find it easy not to build a brick wall because it's not an issue: and it's the same with smoking. I don't find it easy to not smoke - it's just not an issue.

In conclusion, the issue as to whether it's easy to not smoke is in itself one of the illusions of addiction. It isn't easy to not smoke, it isn't anything. While there is a debate in your mind you are not free from the addiction. Whether you are smoking or not is not really relevant to the issue of addiction. Addiction is concerned with whether or not you are still suffering the illusions of addiction. Smoking itself is simply the physical expression of the addiction that exists inside your mind. It's what's called 'active addiction' where you are expressing that addiction by outside physical behaviour.

'Active' & 'Inactive' Addiction

In the previous section I explained that smoking is the physical expression of the addiction, and this is called 'active' addiction. I hope you have understood by now that the addiction is in your mind, and it is about this internal dialogue, or debate, and the feelings of fear and panic caused by this debate. The addiction isn't smoking. It isn't alcohol, drugs, food, gambling, sex etc. These things are simply the expression of the addiction as witnessed by the outside world, they are the consequences and they, in turn, have their own consequences on health, finance and relationships. What causes us to choose our active addictions are the perceived pay-offs. With narcotic drugs there are common payoffs such as numbing the pain. Food, sex and gambling distract from the pain, and smoking also psychologically distracts from the pain. Other payoffs include peer (and therefore self) acceptance - *if I do this, I will fit in* - and the various functions of the addiction such as: food lessens the pain of hunger; alcohol gives me confidence; gambling will make me rich; and smoking helps me relax, concentrate, stay slim, be seen to be cool, cope, feel better, makes eating, sex, drinking, and going to the toilet better.

The payoffs become needs. When the payoffs become needs the panic at the threat of removing the active addiction (drugs, alcohol, smoking etc) ensues. Our internal addiction cannot see that we don't need this drug to function. The loss of the payoffs is too big a loss – even sometimes at the cost of a shortened life. The consequence of a shortened life is acceptable because life's not that great anyway for many people - not that valuable. This is a self-esteem issue, there is help out there, I am not going to go into this.

You will stop smoking painlessly when you no longer have any payoffs. The good news about smoking is, all of the perceived payoffs are illusions. There are no payoffs to smoking. Even the peer acceptance is false, because in reality no-one gives a damn if you smoke or not. The problem with the smoking payoffs is that, though they are all individually illusions, there are so many of them, there exists in our minds a complex interplay of payoffs/illusions and it is like trying to untangle a plate of spaghetti.

Sometimes, people who have been addicted to a particular drug or behaviour manage to stop. When this happens, the addiction is classed as being 'inactive'. Notice, it is not classed as 'gone', or 'over'. The plate of spaghetti in our minds is the addiction and this can never be erased. That is why it is said, *once an addict, always an addict*. By untangling this spaghetti, surely we are removing it? No. What we are doing is attaching conscious thoughts of truth and resolution on to each strand. For example, a strand that says smoking helps me concentrate is taken to a new set of thoughts that assure us this is an illusion which we have picked up because . . . The original illusion is still there in our minds, on the same plate, tangled up with the rest of the plate. All that needs to happen is for one of those strands/thoughts to not find the truth and the addict is once again in some turmoil, and this usually ends up in a return to active addiction. My method of dealing with these thought strands means that this never has to happen.

If the addict does not know how to connect a particular addiction thought/illusion to a set of new thoughts of truth and resolution, then there is turmoil - but sometimes this can be suppressed and the addict does not return to active addiction. Alcoholics call this *'white knuckling it'* - they are not drinking, but they're not happy about it either. Many smokers also do this, it is called *'the willpower method'*, and they are the sort of ex-smokers we have talked about in earlier sections.

The point of this course is to make your addiction inactive completely, rather than inactive only in its outside expression. This means you continue to use the processes given to you in the exercises until every single addiction thought/illusion can find its truth and resolution. Not all thoughts/illusions are covered in this course; it is up to you to seek your answers using the techniques that have been given. If you can resolve one single addiction thought/illusion, you can resolve them all! When this is done there are no more cravings, desires, fears, twinges or longings.

Challenges

In this section we will look at some more of the pitfalls and problems that can arise after you have stopped smoking. By the end of the section you will have a way of dealing with any situations that may arise to challenge you so you can move forward without fear.

After you have had your last cigarette you will be challenged in all kinds of ways, so in the next few sections we are going to have a look at some of the more common challenges life may present. The specific situation may not apply to you, but you will see the process that is used to deal with them, the process that you will be able to apply to the challenges that do come your way. The first challenge we are going to look at is that of partners or family members who smoke.

My partner/family smokes

Living with someone who smokes can seem to be a major problem and certainly there are issues that need to be addressed in order to work through this. Some fundamental questions need to be answered.

Should that person be allowed to smoke in front of you at all?
Should that person be allowed to smoke in the house?
Should that person leave their cigarettes lying around?
Will that person try to get you back smoking?
Will you want your house smelling of smoke now that you are free?

What are your rights and what are the smoker's rights?
Do you personally have a choice in these matters?

Clearly, this issue throws up a lot of questions. If more than one of the people you live with smokes then it may be difficult or impossible to make demands on them. If you can ask them to help you for a time by not smoking right in front of you, not leaving their cigarettes lying, around or not offering you any, then that's fine and reasonable for a couple of days. Beyond that it would be in your best interest to not make an issue of it.

If you live with one person then maybe it is time to look at your rights regarding your shared living space and the health issues, the smell etc. There are no firm right or wrong answers but generally these days, the non-smoker has the moral high ground and you should be able to live in a place that isn't filled with smoke and dirty ashtrays all the time. There are always ways round and negotiations to be made, and this is all part of the rich tapestry of life in relationships.

The fundamental issue that concerns us right now is that you no longer smoke, and the fear is that if you have to live with smoke in the air and cigarettes lying around, you might be tempted to smoke. For what reason? If you have a reason to smoke then you will smoke regardless of anything your partner may or may not do. You have to take responsibility for this. A cigarette is only ever a short walk or drive away at the shop or garage, it can never be someone else's fault for tempting you.

One of the illusions around nicotine addiction as we have seen is that it is the power of the drug nicotine that compels people to smoke. This is absolute nonsense. You partner's second-hand cigarette smoke can not get you back smoking. That is just you blaming something outside of yourself because you think you want or need a smoke, because you are not using the process you have learned to seek the illusion behind your thoughts and feelings. It's got nothing to do with them or the smoke in the air or the cigarettes lying around. The smoke in the air, if it is thick and you have been in it for a long time could possibly cause some withdrawal feelings. They won't wake you from your sleep but it might be possible to notice them if you try especially hard. Those withdrawal feelings cannot compel you to smoke, it is only the illusions you have had that can compel and you have a process to deal with them now.

It is fact that millions of people have stopped smoking even if other members of their family continue to smoke in front of them in the house just. Nicotine is an extremely weak drug and, providing you don't have the addiction illusions, it cannot cause you to want to smoke again. For the first few days, while you are undergoing a change, while you are learning to feel safe without smoking then maybe it can be helpful to have other's consideration, but it is not vital. You have to face the fact that many people do smoke and they will smoke in front of you. They will offer you cigarettes, so you might as well get used to it from the word go. You do not need to hate smoking to be free. In fact, you need to not hate smoking to be genuinely free, because hating smoking is a fight and it is a fight you might lose, so don't go there. Other people smoke. It is unfortunate they are in the grip of all these illusions, but it is not your job to shame them or show them or help them unless they ask you directly. Helping others will not keep you smoke free, it doesn't work that way.

Work

It is the break times at work that can seem to be the biggest challenge, particularly in those first few days of not smoking. If you have been able to smoke any time at work, dealing with your smoking colleagues is pretty much the same as dealing with smoking friends, and these issues are covered in the next sections. But if you work in a no smoking environment you are presented with the dilemma of whether to continue to go to the smoke room/toilet/back entrance with your work friends even though you don't smoke any more. Those break times are when you nurture friendships. It isn't the smoking aspect that is important here, it's the missing out on chatting to your friends. Again, these issues are dealt with in the next section 'All my friends smoke'. Another fear at work is:-

I might miss out on all the gossip if I no longer go into the smoke room with my work colleagues.

You have two choices with this one. Either you don't go there any more or you go there so that you don't miss out on any gossip. When I say 'gossip' I don't mean to be derogatory in any way. It is often socially important to keep up with the news on the grapevine. The important point is that you do actually have the choice. You are free from your addition. Going into the smoke room will not cause you to want to smoke at all. More likely you will feel sick and disgusted because of all the smoke.

All my friends smoke

The fact that many of your friends smoke can be frightening when you are considering stopping smoking. Some friends will support you and some friends will actually try and get you to smoke again in all kinds of subtle and not so subtle ways. The question is, how are you going to be with your friends who are smoking when you're the only one not smoking? Feelings may arise that you are now different, leading to fears that you may be left out or have problems being accepted. You may in fact feel a little superior yourself because you are free from the addiction and your friends may well experience feelings of jealousy towards you. So there are potential causes of friction between yourself and your friends when you stop smoking.

It is very easy to say that this is not an important issue because I come first and my health, finances, kids or whatever comes before my friends, but these fears of being left out, of being a different person are still there. Another fear is that of being asked for advice as to how to do it, and how you have done it, and that if you try to encourage them they may take that as criticism and develop a resentment towards you. For example, if they ask you how you have done it and you suggest they work through this course, if they don't and they continue to smoke, they may well feel resentful: this is human nature.

Here are quite a number of potential problems. Underlining them all is the problem of rejection and abandonment. These are very sensitive issues, particularly to our sub-conscious selves. Abandonment and rejection are one of a human being's greatest fears. The prospect of rejection by one's friends because you are successful in quitting smoking may seem a rather pathetic fear consciously, but sub-consciously it is a huge fear. It is vital to our basic survival that we work as a team, therefore on the primeval level abandonment, is actually life threatening. Fear of abandonment is genetically programmed in our brains from birth. Just the threat of the possibility of abandonment is enough to stimulate an adrenaline reaction, i.e. panic. This panic is wrongly identified by addicts as 'withdrawal' and it is for this reason it is important that we work through this issue.

People who smoke tend to attract people who smoke and non-smokers tend to attract other non-smokers. So when you stop smoking, there is a genuine threat of rejection and abandonment by your group of friends who smoke. In order to become free from this addiction we need to be very, very clear and very specific about this issue. We need to see a definite way through and we need to know exactly what we are going to do, the position we are going to take in relation to our friends who smoke.

What are the options? You can dump all your friends who smoke and stick with the non-smoking friends and get new friends who don't smoke, or, and this is a realistic and valid choice, you can keep all your friends regardless of whether they smoke or not. I mentioned earlier that some of your smoking friends will try and get you to smoke again. They are not nasty, it is just that most addicts do this. You may not but many do, they can't help it. Part of them feels abandoned and rejected by you simply because you have stopped smoking. That is not your fault, it has got nothing to do with you personally and you are powerless over what they think and feel. But if you are aware of what they may be feeling, you can make allowances for them and understand their reactions. Some of the things they say may not seem very nice but you can understand and you will not take anything personally. It is part of their addiction that they try to get you smoking again. They are driven by their fears and one of their fears is that now you are a non-smoker you have become different and the next thing you may do is abandon and reject them. Another of their fears is that because of your success they are not as good as you, not as strong as you, so they must be weaker than, less than. This feeling in them, which has nothing to do with you, can motivate them to react towards you in certain fear-based, defensive ways. You have stopped smoking, they have failed to stop smoking: they are failures and you are now better than them. Many people, particularly addicts it has to be said, suffer from low self-esteem.

This will pass. People will get used to the fact that you are free, they just need some time. The funny thing is, in time some people will forget that you ever smoked. In years to come you will hear it expressed, *"you've never smoked have you?"* So all we are talking about here is people's initial reactions. Apart from their feeling of being abandoned, being 'less than', is their ambition to stop themselves, and they want to know how to do it. All smokers want to stop apart from the liars and the loonies. You advising them to read this book is not, to them, information on how to do it. They will perceive that as you trying to sell them something. They want to be able to stop smoking without having to work through a book, and they are going to ask you how to do that. After all, there's no point in them spending the money if you've already read it and can tell them how to do it.

I think it needs to be stressed at this point that none of this may happen. If it does, be aware that one of their motives in challenging you is to test how strong your recovery from this addiction actually is. Is it real? Is it going to last? So quite often they are just testing you, they are not necessarily trying to make you smoke again. Although they may well feel better if you were to smoke, part of their motivation is to find out if this really does work and can they do it. They are going to ask you questions. They are also going to make excuses as to why they have failed to stop smoking themselves, such as *"I wouldn't know what to do with my hands"* and another favourite, *"I stopped once and I lasted six months"*. When someone says this, they are not trying to undermine you, they are simply saying that they will be interested in how you have achieved this if you can do a significantly longer time than six months. Until then they don't know if your recovery is worth anything.

You will of course get people who come up to you to congratulate and encourage, saying things like they hope you continue not to smoke, that you never go back to it, and they will mean it. Sometimes however this can sound patronising and as if they are putting their fears on to you. When you have got to the end of this course, hopefully you will feel that the matter is resolved, and you do not intend to suffer or struggle for weeks or months or years. But many people's image of an ex-smoker is of someone who lives day to day resisting temptation, so be aware that what may sound patronising or even suspicious to you is a result of part of the shared illusion that is addiction. On the other hand, some people are just down right negative, saying things like they will give you three months or it'll end in tears etc. So you may find yourself being defensive and over-sensitive to what people say because of the possibility of hidden messages, downright negativity or because they give you a reason to smoke that you were not prepared for. If this happens then it is an opportunity for you to look at that issue and to work through it. Get a pen and paper if necessary and work it out. Ask yourself why you are having this reaction, what is it you are afraid of?

So what do we do about friends? The simplest answer is to be free from the addiction. It doesn't matter that you no longer smoke. If you want to go to the smoke room at break time with them to talk, then by all means do so. If you prefer not to sit and gossip with them in a smelly smoked-filled room then don't. They will get used to it either way and so will you. As with any change in life there is a period of adjustment and that is to be expected, but be aware this particular period of adjustment will be very short-lived. People adapt to new situations very quickly.

You are now going to do an exercise where you are presented with a number of situations in which you may find yourself. Write down the thoughts and feelings and the processes you will use to stay smoke free. For Example:

1.   Write down a situation as given below.
2.   Note how you imagine you would feel in that situation.
3.   Identify the thoughts.
4.   Identify any addiction illusions that are behind those thoughts and write down why they are illusions.
5.   Write down what will happen if you smoke and what will happen if you don't smoke.

SITUATIONS

The situations are:-

1.   Going to the cinema with friends.

2.   Going out for a meal with family and/or friends.

3.   Attending a wedding.

4.   Having a break at work where my friends have to go outside to smoke.

5.   Having a break at work where my friends have to go to the smoke-room.

6.   Having a smoking friend or friends visiting me at my house.

7.   Going out for a drink with friends.

8.   Going clubbing with friends.

Here is an example answer:-

1.   *SITUATION: Playing cards with friends.*
2.   *I imagine I would feel apprehensive and self conscious.*
3.   *I would be worried that seeing my friends smoke in front of me would make me want to smoke too. I would be afraid of them asking me if I wanted a cigarette because then I would*

have to explain I had given up. I might not be able to concentrate properly. I wouldn't know what to do with my hands and I would feel too insecure to bluff and hide my feelings, I would feel exposed.

4.   *ILLUSION: I want to smoke – no I don't! ILLUSION: They will reject me now I'm a non smoker – they don't really care and this will pass very soon anyway. ILLUSION: smoking helps me concentrate – in reality it hinders concentration. ILLUSION: fiddling with a cigarette helps me bluff and protects me emotionally – I can fiddle with the cards, chips, snacks, my hair, my collar, my ears, my mouth, my drink etc etc etc.*

5.   *If I smoke I will hate myself, lose my friend's respect, become a slave again and be even more afraid and addicted. If I don't smoke, that situation will never be a problem again.*

The purpose of this exercise is to make sure that you are not going into anxiety producing situations unprepared when you have stopped smoking. Completing this exercise fully will ensure that you do not fear situations, and your mind is set up to reinforce your new beliefs with each situation that comes along.

Getting drunk

This exercise probably raised the issue of *what happens when I get drunk?* The fear is that *if I get drunk I will not have control and my resistance will be low. Also, drink and smoking go together and I don't know if I can enjoy a drink without a smoke and the more drink I have, the more likely I will end up smoking. I know loads of people who started smoking again because they got drunk.*

There are millions of people who have successfully become free from this addiction and have got drunk many times yet not gone back to smoking. There are also people who have got drunk and gone back to smoking. There's no illusion going on here is there? Well maybe there is. When I get drunk I lose my inhibitions and I do things I want to do in an unrestrained way, without really thinking about it. But really, I do know what I'm doing. I may not have very good recall of it the next day, but while I'm doing what I'm doing when I'm drunk I do really know what I'm doing. What I can do is blame being drunk for my current behaviour.

So you get drunk, smoke and blame it on being drunk. What happens next morning when you are no longer drunk? You still blame being drunk. You say that you got drunk and smoked yesterday and that is why you are smoking today. This is typical behaviour for an addict. To blame being afraid or anxious about something which may happen in the future or something that happened in the past for your present behaviour. It is not getting drunk that causes ex-smokers to smoke, it is just a convenient excuse to stop suffering. If you are not suffering in the first place you will not smoke just because you are drunk just as you won't build a brick wall just because you are drunk. If you are suffering, then yes, getting drunk is an ideal way to find an excuse to stop the suffering, but we are not stopping smoking and suffering; we have become free, so getting drunk has no effect one way or the other. There simply is no reason to use being drunk as an excuse to do something we know we should not do in order to stop the suffering we are not actually suffering from. Do you see?

There is no question of our resistance being low when we are drunk. This can only arise if you are actually resisting something. We are not learning how to resist smoking, building walls or whatever, we are becoming free by seeing the truth. Getting drunk cannot take away knowledge and the awareness of truth. It tends to do the opposite; people tend to get a little over truthful when they get drunk. Someone who is free from this addiction does not get drunk and smoke. They get drunk and then tell people who do smoke about all the illusions they are really suffering from. *"I luv yooo. A'll tell yooo a shecret shll'I? Shmokin ish $£!%*!"*

If you are not free from this addiction and you still have some issues that you are reluctant to work through then getting drunk may well lead to you smoking again – because you are not free, you are still suffering. Here is a subtle trap. How do you know when there are no issues at all left for you to work out? Until you know the answer to this question then surely, getting drunk is a risk. This is another addiction illusion. Behind it is the idea that drink and smoking go together. This idea is complete nonsense and the only reason it seems to be true is that you may well have never experienced drink while being free from this addiction. Maybe you are one of those fortunate people who can remember a time when they used to drink and got drunk before they started smoking. If you are, then it is possible for you to recall that you enjoyed drinking just as much when you didn't smoke. For a great many people, drinking and smoking happened at about the same time or smoking happened before any serious drinking. So the illusion that drinking and smoking go together is very strong, but you have to recognise that people who don't smoke enjoy a drink just as much as people who do. Ex-smokers also enjoy a drink and they don't start smoking again because of it.

There is another illusion that comes with drinking. Cigarettes seem to taste better and they seem to be more enjoyable. They seem to taste better because the sugar in the drink takes away the nasty taste of the cigarettes and because the alcohol acts like an anaesthetic to numb the effects of the toxic smoke you are inhaling. They seem to be more enjoyable because the alcohol takes away your inhibitions. This takes away the fear of the health risks and the guilt about what you are doing to yourself in terms of health and finance, low self esteem and the self disgust that every addict feels about their slavery and their failure to break free. The cigarettes don't really taste nicer when you drink and they are not more enjoyable, it is all just addiction illusions.

Going back to the earlier issue of the subtle trap. Addiction relies on fear. Fear relies on lack of truth or knowledge and illusions. If getting drunk is a fear then to work through that issue you need to identify why it is a fear. We have already done this. Getting drunk is a fear because of the combined illusions that ex-smokers who get drunk go back smoking: drinking and smoking go together and you lose control when you are drunk which must mean that you will smoke. Maybe there are more illusions about this for you to work through. There is one other illusion about drinking leading you to smoke again that you need to be aware of. It is to do with the fear. If you avoid getting drunk because you are afraid of smoking then one day you will get drunk and you will smoke. The very best thing to do is get drunk as soon as you feel secure, i.e. next week. That way you are not living in fear of getting drunk and smoking. If you get drunk intentionally to work through this fear you will not smoke and thereafter you will be free to get drunk any time you wish without living in fear of it leading you to smoke again. The fear of getting drunk and smoking is an addiction illusion and it is an addiction fear.

Something really bad happens

Let's say you find yourself in a situation in which you've had a period of time not smoking; you haven't particularly had a great deal of debate about it in your mind; you've not been suffering in any way, and you've dealt with most of your illusions. Then something happens. Something happens in life as it often does. For example, someone close to you dies. You are at the hospital in the waiting room, you have just been told the news and the nurse says, "do *you want a cigarette*?" You reply that you gave up six months ago and the nurse says this is not the time for giving up and hands you a lit cigarette. It is at this particular point that you would expect to be vulnerable. You would think, "*well yes, under those circumstances it's understandable that I'd probably pick up that cigarette.*" That would certainly seem the easier course of action. Let me warn you now, it is not the easier course of action. It is very much the hardest course of action.

Whoever just died does not want you to do that. I'm sure that person would care more about you than to want you to pick up that cigarette. We have dealt with the stories of smokers and ex-smokers; they are people not to be trusted with regard to this issue of nicotine addiction. Smokers are not to be trusted because they are in it and some ex-smokers are not to be trusted because although they may not be smoking, they still suffer from the illusions that make up addiction. In that hospital waiting room taking the cigarette from the nurse is the hard way, it's not the easy way. The easy way is to ask the question: *why would I want to smoke a cigarette? Because I used to smoke? That's not a reason to smoke. Because someone else is assuming I cannot cope with a situation without some form of drug? Will the cigarette help me cope with this situation;, do I go back into that lie that cigarettes help you cope with anything? The truth is the cigarette cannot help me cope; it can only hinder my ability to cope by increasing my physical responses and trigger more emotions; as if I hadn't got enough already.*

So even when you think you are free, now and again life can present you with challenges. That is the thing about life. Whenever you think you've got something sorted out it tends to rear it's head up to you and say, *"Oh yeah! You think you're sorted? Well try this for size!"* and it tests you and challenges you. You will be challenged if you have uncertainty and doubt and these are opportunities for you to resolve the issue or illusion you may still hold. Decide now! Under no circumstances and not for ANY reason is it easier to smoke. It's easier to work it through and to let it go so it is no longer an issue. So when somebody says, *"do you want a cigarette?"* in some particularly

267

difficult or distressing situation, it is easier to say *"I don't smoke"* rather than *"I gave up"*. When you say you have given up, you are inviting a possible debate from that person. If you are inviting a debate from that person then you must also be inviting a debate in your own mind which suggests that there is more to debate in your own mind, and you will lose because you are in a distressing situation and it is the wrong time to enter into a debate. But this isn't going to happen to you. This is what happens to people who do not know that addiction is a set of thoughts that fire off a set of feelings and that the answer to it is to deal with those thoughts. To identify what those thoughts are, have a look at them, hold them up to the light to see if they have any validity whatsoever or any truth in them. You know to do that and you know how to do it because you have been taught by working through this course, so you are not going to find yourself in this situation. You are going to find that not smoking is as easy as not building a brick wall. You've looked at the illusions, you've worked through all the reasons there are to smoke and you have seen that it is all complete and utter nonsense. Those addiction thoughts and feelings cannot come back to haunt you or to get you at times when you're vulnerable because you have dealt with them already. You have looked at them. You are not afraid of them when they do turn up because you have a process to deal with them. And you know what; they know that too, so they don't bother turning up, even in vulnerable situations.

Nothing happens

Life has its ups and downs and we react with various feelings. If you are an addict, the very next thought after a feeling is that a drug will temporarily and partially relieve you of having to feel that feeling. The next thought is that if you don't have that drug then you will feel even worse. By now, the addict has forgotten what the feeling was about in the first place and can only see that the feeling is about withdrawal and therefore the drug will completely solve it. This addiction process has occurred in your brain approximately seventy three thousand times if you have smoked for ten years. It is only natural therefore that it will occur a few times after you have stopped smoking and you are no longer withdrawing. See the process for what it is – a lie that generates fear. By having this awareness you can no longer be controlled by this process.

I just want one!

It's not that it is easy to not smoke, it's just that it's not there. There's nothing there to be easy about. What happens, let's say, the day after you had your last cigarette around two-thirty in the afternoon and you have this terrible, awful feeling that you really do need to smoke now, that your life depends on it, you have to have a smoke and you can feel your choice in the matter slipping away with this incredible compulsion? You go through your process. You identify the physical symptoms of the feelings to detach, and then you look for the thought behind it. What if, after spending five minutes looking for this thought the only answer you can come up with is, *"'cos I want one!"* You can say to yourself that you don't really want one because you don't want to be a smoker: I really want to not smoke, I want to be free from this addiction, that's what I really want. But you can want to be free from the addiction and still feel you want to have a cigarette right now this minute. Your current bottom line is, *"I just want to have one smoke, that's all, I just want one!"* Let's have a look at this.

When you get to the stage of saying there is no underlying reason behind this feeling, behind this compulsion behind this overwhelming desire. The only reason behind it that I can come up with is that I want one, *I just want one, sod this I don't want to argue about it any more I'm sick of it, I'm sick of this debate, the bottom line is I just want one.* You may be fully aware that you don't really want one, that you're just a victim of the illusion that if you don't have one you will go nuts. You may be fully aware that something has triggered this panic attack, this compulsion, and that you have just been unable to find out what it is. That is what, *"I just want one"* means. It means you cannot find the thought behind this feeling (or the thoughts). Maybe there are too many thoughts all ganging up on me or maybe it's just a thought that we haven't covered in the course; or it's just an elusive thought right now at this particular moment for whatever reason. When you can't find the thought behind the feeling there are a number of thoughts that come up to cover that failure. One is, *"I just want one"* another is, *"I just can't carry on"* another one is, *"I need to do more work, maybe I need to work through the course again"*. These kinds of thoughts become reasons to smoke. They are cover-up thoughts. They disguise the thoughts that are actually creating your current state of feelings and your current state of mind. You cannot identify the real thoughts so these are the sorts of thoughts that come up. You've had these thoughts many times before, probably whenever you have tried to stop smoking, and they are the last thoughts of desperation before the next cigarette.

This is all perfectly natural. Yes, it is insane but it is a very common insanity, its called addiction. It doesn't make you any less of a person, it's just one of those processes of addiction whereby you cannot find any reasons to indulge in the addiction but the feelings are very compelling and in order to act out on the addiction you have these all-embracing cover-up thoughts that don't in themselves mean anything. *"I want one. I can't fight this any more. I've had enough. I'm throwing the towel in. I just can't do it. It's too early in the morning for me to fight this thing. I'll tackle this another day."* Most people, when they've worked through this course do not get to this point, they do not suffer this horrendous compulsion, this feeling of weakness, this feeling of less than, this feeling of being defeated. But some people do go through such periods of difficulty and it is only natural that this is experienced by some. It is not something to beat yourself up about or to consider yourself as less than, or a failure. One thought that arises when faced with this kind of difficulty immediately after stopping smoking is, *"Well if I am feeling this way and having so much difficulty locating what the thought is behind this feeling, then obviously I haven't understood something."* There's no getting by that. Clearly I haven't understood something or otherwise I wouldn't be having this difficulty, this feeling, thinking I just want one when I know I don't, or I can't cope when I know there's nothing to cope with. Clearly there's something going on, something inside saying *"I have already failed at this"*. You don't need to pick up a cigarette to fail, what's happening in your mind is *"you have already failed"*. You are feeling this feeling and you are having difficulty finding the thought behind the feeling, therefore you have not understood today, you have failed, game over, we'll have a cigarette and have another go another day.

Game Over?

It is at this point, at this moment of fear and panic, terror and confusion that you win or lose. This is the important point. Yes, there's something you've not understood; yes, you can't find that thought right now because you are full of these feelings, and yes, it's bloody awful. So how do you deal with this? How do you tackle this moment in time? I will now show you exactly what you can do that works. Once you have reached this thoroughly hopeless moment when there is no longer any point trying to work it out or deal with the issues, it's time to apply a new thought. You can think the thought or repeat it out loud as many times as you like. The thought is:-

"These feelings and this confusion will pass whether I smoke or not."

If I smoke it will pass, if I don't smoke it will pass. In time I will understand what's behind these feelings if I smoke now - and in time I will understand what's behind these feelings if I don't smoke now. If I smoke I am guaranteeing that I will re-experience these feelings and this confusion time and time and time again. If I don't smoke I am guaranteeing that this is the last time I will suffer these feelings and this confusion. If you do not pick up a cigarette at this point it is the last time you feel those awful feelings. Why? Because afterwards, when those feelings have gone, you will be able to think about what happened and you'll probably find the reason. Even if you don't find the reason it might have just been a habitual kind of panic attack. Or you might sort out the reason another way and not even notice; the mind is a very complex thing. You can have a thought that creates tremendous feelings of panic one day and then you can deal with that thought later not even knowing that's the thought that created the previous panic. One way or another you will work through every addiction thought. You have no choice; that's what you have learned to do having worked through this course.

Is this easy? Nobody is trying to pretend that these panic situations are easy. They may well not come up, but if they do then certainly they couldn't be described as being easy times. But neither could they be honestly described as impossible times. It is certainly possible to win through because millions have already successfully coped and you now have the tools to do so too.

Now please say out loud six times – just do it!

> **These** *feelings and this confusion will pass whether I smoke or not.*
> *These feelings and this confusion* **will** *pass whether I smoke or not.*
> *These feelings and this confusion will* **pass** *whether I smoke or not.*
> *These feelings and this confusion will pass* **whether** *I smoke or not.*
> *These feelings and this confusion will pass whether* **I** *smoke or not.*
> *These feelings and this confusion will pass whether I smoke* **or not.**

Curiosity

If after my last cigarette, I no longer have any reason to smoke, like 'it tastes nice' or 'it helps me relax' etc, then surely after a while of not smoking I might be able to have the occasional smoke like other people do? - The problem with this idea is that it is a lie. You are saying you have no reason to smoke yet you are thinking of having a smoke. You claim there is no reason to smoke so why on earth would you consider having a smoke.

Answer – *To prove I am no longer addicted.* This is a compelling reason to smoke once you have stopped, to prove that it can no longer have such a terrible hold on you. So you do have a reason to smoke!

Admission of powerlessness is the answer. What does this mean? In Alcoholics Anonymous and other Anonymous groups they have a thing called 'Step One'. Step one says *"We admitted we were powerless over alcohol/gambling/our addiction and that our lives had become unmanageable."* This step one has obvious meaning and a whole host of deeper meanings. If you can have some grasp of what it means you will not have any desire to smoke occasionally or try one out of curiosity because you will have admitted that you are powerless over nicotine. What does it mean to admit you are powerless over nicotine? Well put very simply, it means that once you have put nicotine into your system you then have no control over whether or when you will be able to stop doing it. It means you are admitting that the way the drug affects you means you have little or no control. It means that once you put the drug into your system it triggers a whole, complex set of thoughts and addictive behaviours over which you have no real control. In other words, you are taking your life into your hands by putting that drug into your system. If you truly accept that this is the truth, then it is a massive risk to try it just for the sake of curiosity, to think you might be able to control it this time after years of it controlling you is not a sane thought. To sum up, you just accept that you are powerless over nicotine, or you are powerless over the addiction process that nicotine sets off in you. Admitting that you personally are powerless ends the argument about whether to try a smoke or not for any reason. That is not to say anybody else is powerless, all you are admitting is that you are powerless.

Remember a time

There was a very long period in your life when you did not smoke. You did not miss smoking. You knew the truth that you did not need to smoke. You just didn't think about it one way or another. It may have been a long time ago, but I would like you to remember that time before you smoked, before smoking or not smoking became an issue. Just take a minute to go back there in your imaginations.

Most of the things you do in life today, you did then. You woke each morning, you ate, you went to the toilet, you concentrated, you relaxed, you coped with everything life threw at you and you didn't once have the thought that you needed a cigarette. Yes, but that was before you became addicted I hear you thinking, things have changed so it's not the same now. Being able to remember a time when you were able to cope and relax without a smoke can be helpful, so let's deal with the idea that things have changed. What exactly has changed? You were not addicted and now you are.

If nicotine is addictive then it was addictive when you didn't smoke; nothing has changed there. You not smoking did not make nicotine any less or more addictive than it is or isn't now. If you are addicted because you have smoked then clearly the only thing that has changed is that you have smoked. If you choose to stay smoke free then you will cease to be addicted just as before. Maybe it's nothing to do with addiction. Maybe it is to do with your conscious illusions that smoking is needed to cope, or that it is a pleasure you would be missing and you didn't know that before you took up smoking. Maybe that's the real difference. So why did you start smoking? It is highly probable that before you started smoking you had already bought into the beliefs that smoking was a pleasure and it helped cope with stress. Since in reality it does neither of these things you had to have these beliefs already in place in order for the cigarettes to do these things and even then you had to work at it initially. At first you had to keep having a go to make smoking appear to do for you what your beliefs told you it should do. You had to have these illusions before you smoked. Nothing has changed there. This clearly explains why people find it difficult to stop and stay stopped. They still have the same beliefs and illusions they had before they ever started smoking.

So what has changed? Fear. Before you smoked, you did not fear not smoking, after you smoked you did fear not smoking. Let's just remind ourselves once again where this fear comes from. You decide not to smoke anymore and this creates a little understandable anxiety. A minuscule amount of adrenaline is produced and this creates physical sensations. These in turn produce an anxious feeling so more adrenaline is produced. There is a cascade effect and all we know about it is that we go from anxiety to fear to terror to panic. The key to this process is ignorance. If you know what is happening and why, then the depth of the anxiety is mostly removed and this awareness stops the fear to panic process. It is this that has changed now.

Trying to remember a time when the issue of smoking or not smoking was not in your life at all simply means remembering a time before the debate about whether to smoke or not appeared, usually it is in our mid teens. The actual act of smoking does not really come into it one way or the other.

Meditation - How it works

In this section there is a full explanation of the use of meditation as a tool with regard to becoming free. By the end of this section you will have knowledge of the benefits of short-term meditation and you will have recorded a meditation for you to use in preparation for the time you have stopped smoking.

Before we move on to the last cigarette it is a good idea to prepare a meditation. If the whole idea of meditation is unfamiliar to you, you may well feel some anxiety about this, maybe even some hostility. Doing the work I will be asking of you in this section will give you another tool to help you become free and it is well worth the effort, but I also have to say that it is not absolutely essential to do this part. You can be just as free, just as easy by missing out this part if you feel uncomfortable with it or do not have the resources to hand. You can record a meditation on tape or CD for you to play back to yourself when you have stopped smoking. You can use this meditation as many times as you wish, though most only use it for a short time, rarely more than a few weeks and mostly just a few days. If the thought of recording your own voice is too uncomfortable to you then you can purchase a recording of the meditation at www.StopSmokingPlan.org

Is it Hypnotism? Well, the guided meditation we are going to do could be seen as being close to hypnosis, but that's not really it. Working through this course is an attempt to alter fundamental beliefs about a particular, distinct subject. Part of that process involves trying to touch, or get through to the sub-conscious by working through beliefs and yes, even a little meditation. Guided meditation and hypnosis are similar, but hypnosis induces a state of trance in which conscious barriers are temporarily suspended. A trance is not necessary in this particular process because the key to freedom is conscious awareness.

It is possible to be in a form of trance in guided meditation and the lines between meditation and trance are probably not always distinct. Trance aside, hypnosis and meditation and working through beliefs are powerful techniques. My friend went to a hypnotist to try to stop smoking. I hasten to add at this point that hypnosis works in different ways and I have no idea of the success rate hypnotists have with regard to smoking cessation. My approach is very. As I said, my friend saw a hypnotist. He put her in a trance and made her sub-conscious believe that cigarettes tasted so foul and obnoxious there was no way she could stand the taste. Sure enough, for a few weeks, every time she lit a cigarette, it tasted so foul to her she instantly put it out. Eventually however, she managed to work through this and she was back on twenty a day. This doesn't mean that the hypnosis failed, it just means that that it was, in a very simplistic way, trying to deal with a symptom, rather than the problem. When smokers first begin smoking, we do find the taste pretty foul. But after a short while the addiction process kicks in and our brains then need to get over the foul taste. It does this so successfully we can even come to believe that a foul tasting cigarette actually tastes nice. My friend's brain had already been through the process of getting her to believe that foul tasting smoke tastes nice. After the hypnosis it simply went through the same process again.

Addiction is powerful and complex and it relies on conscious beliefs to support it as well as sub-conscious issues and beliefs. To be free, you have to work through beliefs that have kept you stuck and acquire new beliefs that will set you free and keep you free. This is what we are doing with this course.

Let me give you a real life example of how powerful new beliefs can be. There was a TV documentary some years ago about a surgeon; I think he works in Italy, who performs operations without using anaesthetic. It followed a woman who needed an operation to remove varicose veins in her legs. This is very painful for the patient even after they come out of the anaesthetic, let alone having the operation without anaesthetic altogether. The surgeon changes the patient's beliefs about pain through hypnosis and conscious reason. There are many examples of human beings overcoming physical pain through willpower or faith. Such as firewalkers and Hindu Kaffirs who lie on beds of nails etc. They have a technique, a belief, a thought pattern that allows them to block out the pain. It is true, and it works. This surgeon's particular technique is to give his patients this belief. When a person experiences physical pain, their mouths turn dry. It is one of our body's physical responses to the sensation of pain. If you block this response then you will block the sensation of pain. So by focussing your mind on producing and maintaining saliva in your mouth, then you simply cannot feel any pain. It actually works. This lady was trained in less than half an hour to do this and the surgeon then tested her by sticking needles into her and she didn't even flinch. Once she was convinced of her new power she underwent the operation without any anaesthetic and she was back at work the same afternoon. Personally, I thought she was nuts. I would have taken a fortnight off sick for that at the very least! But the point is this. By working through the conscious and sub-conscious beliefs you can change your mind about anything. It is very powerful and it works. Decide right now that being free from your nicotine addiction is certainly possible and it is easy. If you mind has just thrown up any contradictory thoughts then write them down now. Freedom from nicotine addiction is easy. Write down any thoughts that come up, don't question them, just write them down.

The next step is to record the following guided meditation. The first part is the instructions that you give yourself to prepare for the meditation. The second part is the meditation itself. You record both parts. You can also record it with relaxing music in the background or just play relaxing music while you are actually meditating, providing it is very quiet. The meditation itself, including the instruction, takes about twenty minutes. The very best way is to record this yourself as if you are your own parent or a teacher or guide. Leave plenty of gaps and spaces and silences for understanding and for pictures to be able to form in your mind. Another way is to have a supportive person read it out to you. Alternatively you can purchase a recording of the meditation from Release for Life. In the next section it is a good idea to do this meditation straight after you have smoked your last cigarette.

Meditation – child cloud

We are going to have a brief meditation. This is not hypnotism, you are not going into a trance and you cannot accidentally fall into a trance. The purpose of this meditation is to help your deep sub-conscious accept the idea of freedom from addiction to nicotine. To give a part of you support and comfort in this process.

Quite naturally, you are bound to feel somewhat anxious or nervous about something so unfamiliar to you. However, if you go with this willingly you will soon feel ok and very relaxed. You may even fall asleep. During this meditation, you have to give me permission to take you on a journey, to challenge your belief. Before we begin, you need to give me permission to enter your protected zone, your sub-conscious self. If you've never consciously been there before let me assure you here and now that there is nothing to fear there. You cannot be harmed in any way. The experience will be a changing experience and that means you will not be the same person you were before the meditation. You will be a different person. You will have been changed from deep within in a very specific way about a specific issue. There will exist deep within you an idea, a concept of letting go, with love, of your addiction to nicotine. It's not the be all and end all. It's just yet another part of the whole complex process. Give me permission to take you there, you have nothing to fear. The first thing is to get physically comfortable in such a way that you could fall asleep. By all means lie on the bed or floor. If you really don't want to lie on the bed or floor then get in a position where you can fall asleep in your chair.

Now that you are comfortable we are going to relax our bodies. If you have an itch, scratch it, if you want to change position at any time, change position. That's all ok, it will not lessen the power of the meditation and even if it does, that's ok too because you can do this as many times as you like, whenever you like.

Now I'd like you to focus on your breathing. Make your breaths slower and longer. Keep focussed on your breathing. As other thoughts come up let them go. Don't try to stop any thoughts coming up, just allow them to drift away and focus your attention on your breathing. Allow your whole body to go limp and heavy. Still concentrate on your breathing. Allow the muscles in your forehead to let go. Allow your eyelids to let go and allow them to drop down without actually shutting. Feel your eyelids becoming heavier and heavier. Keep focussed on your breathing.

Imagine you are in a green field of felt, not grass, but soft green felt. There are low, rolling green felt hills in the distance. The green felt is very soft. The sky is powder blue with fluffy white cotton wool clouds. There are flowers here and there also made of felt, yellow one's and pink one's dotted about here and there. It is sunny and warm and you can faintly hear in the distance the sound of a trickling stream. It is sunny and warm and you feel safe and secure.

There is a young child. A four year old. It is you when you were four. You kneel down by your child and you notice your child playing with a pack of your brand of cigarettes or tobacco. You do not stop your child playing with the pack because in this reality there is only love and acceptance, there is no judgement or anger or control. In this reality there is only pure, unconditional love, peace, joy and acceptance.

You have a shoebox. You show it to your child and you place it on the green felt ground. You take off the lid. Your child understands your intention. In this reality there is a loving God who lives in the heavens. We are going to send God a gift. Your child places the pack of cigarettes or tobacco in the shoe box.

There appears on the ground a roll of giftwrap paper and some cellotape and ribbon and those safety scissors you get in primary school. You place the lid on the shoe box and you help your child wrap the gift. Your child needs your help to cut the paper and wrap the gift and to tie the bow on the ribbon, so help your child to wrap the gift.

When the gift is wrapped you are both pleased and excited. In the distance in the powder blue sky a small cloud approaches. It is low and looks denser and more solid than the other clouds. It finally stops just above and in front of you, just over head height. Your child cannot reach the cloud and needs your help to put his gift in the cloud. You pick up your child and your child places the gift in the cloud. After this, the cloud slowly drifts off and upwards into the powder blue sky. You and your child wave as you watch it slowly float off in the distance, getting smaller and smaller until it disappears.

You and your child hug each other with love and affection. The picture fades. Focus on your breathing. Your eyelids are heavy. Breathe deeper, longer and slower. In . . . and out.

Soon you will be wide awake and you will feel clean and refreshed and full of energy as if your batteries have been re-charged. Your eyelids are getting lighter . . . and lighter. Your eyes open. You are wide awake. Slowly stand up. Move your arms and legs. Feel lighter and clean and refreshed and free.

Part 4

Release

Last Cigarette

During the course of this book we have looked at and worked through just about every issue there is to do with the addiction to nicotine. We have looked at what the addiction is in reality and we have gone into the complexities of this insidious affliction. We have taken apart all the illusions that make up the addiction so that we have become consciously aware of them as illusions and not real. This awareness means that we no longer have to be the victims of such illusions, we now have a choice. We have looked at the physical, emotional and psychological aspects of the sickness of addiction so that whatever happens in the future in terms of thoughts, feelings and physical sensations we know exactly what they are about so we now have much less fear and uncertainty about them. We have looked at the resistances and barriers to freedom such as our own beliefs and illusions and other people, places and things, so they no longer can be insurmountable barriers to our breakout and freedom. We have done exercises both thought repetition and written so that we now have a process by which any thoughts or feelings about smoking can be overcome and used to our advantage. We have faced it all and we have put processes in place to deal with any little thing that comes along that we may have missed.

We are approaching that time when we are going to smoke the last cigarette. At the beginning of this course I asked you to jot down any thoughts or feelings that came up for you during the course of the book. You may have written copious amounts, or you may have forgotten to do this at all or you might have only done it a little – that's ok. You may have made written or mental notes and found that the course has covered them. I would like you to take some time now to have a look at that list and to think about any more issues or problems you still have with anything you have read in this book. Jot down any concerns you still have about stopping smoking and becoming free. Jot down anything you feel you may not fully understand or any uncomfortable feelings, whatever they are. Just spend a few moments to think about this. If there are any un-resolved issues you still have then before going on it is important to completely clear them up. You can go through any relevant sections where you think the answer may be found, something you might have missed. If you have tried this and it hasn't worked then you can re-read the whole book and throughout the course of doing so your answer will probably appear. You can write the issue down and go through the process of identifying the feelings, thoughts and illusions again. Once you have resolved every single issue, then and only then continue and smoke your last cigarette.

Now we have come to that time when we are going to have the last cigarette. What I want you to do is take out a cigarette from the packet and light it. Now I want you to throw away the packet and lighter or matches into a receptacle used for the purpose of removing refuse (bin/trash can). This is to symbolise the throwing away of the addiction from out of your life, the whole thing has now been binned/trashed and cleared away. It is important that you have a last cigarette. The reason for this is that if you don't make a mental note that you are having a last cigarette then you haven't had your last cigarette so you have a reason to smoke - to have your last cigarette. Having your last cigarette removes that reason so it is not floating around in your mind. You can now definitely remember having your last cigarette. You should now read this course to the end. There isn't much left but it will add completeness to the process.

After your last cigarette

After your last cigarette you might think, *"I can't believe it, I don't want to smoke."* Change that immediately to, *"Gosh he was right, I don't want to smoke, I do believe it, I want to keep my freedom"* The reason I say this is because the language you use in your self talk is very important. If you say you don't believe something then you won't believe it whereas if you say you do believe something then you reinforce it and you will believe it.

After your last cigarette you will not want to smoke. You will have no desire to smoke. If any fear or insecurity comes along you will immediately identify it as being the result of a flawed belief, a lie, and it will not defeat you because you will know what it is about. You will know that this feeling is not *"I want a cigarette"*. You will know that this thought of need is mistaken - you simply don't need it to concentrate or relax.

Let us recap once again what are the pleasures of smoking. Relief from actual slight withdrawal, relief from the thought of deprivation, and the belief in the illusions. The first two pleasures can only be experienced by a withdrawing addict and the last two can only be experienced by someone who believes the illusions. Becoming aware of and giving up the illusions takes away the pleasure and need of smoking. In this way you are not giving up smoking, you are simply giving up the illusions. Without the illusions there is no fear and panic to cause the adrenaline that causes the withdrawals. The actual withdrawal from the drug nicotine is so slight you may notice nothing at all, but even if you do, it is only a slight, brief and temporary discomfort, without the illusions and panic it passes in minutes, sometimes seconds. Even if you do experience adrenaline and panic, because you know that this is as a result of a strong illusion you have, you can identify what the feelings are, what the thought and what is the illusion behind it is. So even the adrenaline and panic are now very useful to you because they will compel you to see the lies and the illusions that are strong in you. What if you have done all this and you are still in a panic? Well the truth is you haven't got to the bottom of what the illusion is at the moment or it might be the most subtle illusion of all, that it is necessary to go through a period of physical symptoms and panic in order to be free from this addiction. If that is the case then all you have to do is ask the illusion how long you have to go through this. Once the illusion tells you how long then agree to it and let it be ok and get on with your life.

The reason it is best to simply get on with your life is because any change you make to accommodate giving up smoking is in itself giving credence to illusions and expectations that it is difficult and therefore requires some special attention. If you do not give it special attention you are treating it appropriately in that the actual nicotine withdrawal is so slight it is not worth changing anything to try to accommodate it. So drink your drinks in front of the television as usual. Do your work as usual.

If fear and panic come along in the next few days it is important that you are clear as to why there is fear and panic. After today that fear and panic may not happen at all and if they do you will know exactly what they are and are not about so they cannot have the power over you they used to have. So let us now clearly identify what they are about and what they are not about.

They are there because you have decided not to smoke. All you have to do is to decide to smoke and the fear and panic will leave you. They are not there because of some chemical thing going off in your brain or body. They are not about the fact that you didn't get enough love in your childhood. They are not there because you want to smoke. They are not there because you don't want to give up really. They are not there because of any lack of willpower. They are there because an addiction thought triggered a feeling which caused anxiety which produced adrenaline. There is an issue behind them. Use the process of detaching from the feelings by identifying the physical symptoms, then identify the thought behind the feeling and see the illusion for what it is. Use the truth you have learned off by heart throughout the course of this book:-

"These feelings and this confusion will pass whether I smoke or not."

Don't think about it

Of course it is easy to not do something. I don't do the washing up and I find not doing the washing up really easy. I don't put on a really tight elasticated pair of underpants in order to experience the relief of taking them off again, and I find it really easy not to do that. In fact, it takes no effort on my part at all to not do that. I find it really easy to not inhale a load of toxic fumes in order to relieve the withdrawal feelings I am not experiencing.

It's no problem to me at all. Really. I don't suffer because I have no illusions. My only fear is that I will get captured by enemy agents and be forced to smoke some cigarettes and then I'll be hooked again. No, I'm only kidding. I don't really fear any such thing. I have no illusions. I know there is no pleasure, purpose, relief or need to smoke. I know that having one cigarette means that I will be hooked again because I was never really free from my illusions. If I had been free from my illusions, I wouldn't have had that one cigarette. I am free, I have nothing to prove, I don't need to do any more research in this matter. Smoking is rubbish. This I know after years of research. I get up on a morning, I drink my drink, I eat my breakfast and I get on with my day. I don't suffer. I don't resist any urge to smoke. I don't fear a craving or a desire coming up when I least expect it.

When I was first becoming free, the old feeling came up that at first seemed like a desire or need to smoke. Really, it was a question translated into a feeling. The question was always, *"I have a desire or need to smoke because . . . ?"* Since I already knew the answer was there is never any pleasure in smoking, or need to smoke, I just needed to know what the '. . .' was. For example, a feeling came up - a little bit of panic. Then I asked the question, *"Why do you think we need or want a smoke?"* and the answer was, *"I am totally stressed and a cigarette is the answer to everything. The physical symptoms are extreme tiredness and my neck and chest feels tight and I have a headache and I feel weepy. So, I feel this way because I am stressed. I know it is an illusion that the answer is a cigarette so why do I think it will solve everything? Because I believed smoking would help me relax. Do I believe that now? No, but I don't know how to relax without smoking. Try lying on the couch and watching TV ."* And guess what. That little bit of compromise did the trick and a brief period of slouching was enjoyed without recourse to giving up my freedom.

Anger

Another time a panic came up was a fortnight after my last cigarette. The panic was intense and sudden. I asked myself the question, *"Why do you think we want or need a smoke?"* And the answer was, *"Oh shut the beep up you beeping stupid beeping beep. For beeps sake I'm beeping sick of this, who the beep gives a beep. We don't care any more and I'm not going to discuss it. I'm sick of listening to Mr beeping reasonable, just go and get some."* Five minutes later I was smoking. Another part of me put the cig out after one puff. Another part of me lit another cig. The other part of me put it out, the other part of me lit another, I shouted out, *"Why?"*, I heard back, *"I am angry!"* and I realised that for years, I had dealt with the immediate effects of anger by smoking aggressively. I put out the cigarette and looked for another way to deal with my anger. I couldn't find one. So I just decided to be angry and stay angry. I didn't like it. Smoking seemed like the way to release the tension and allow the movement of the emotion. I decided to trust. I made a decision to trust that sooner or later this would pass and my mind would eventually find a way to deal with the anger in a different way. Later, after the anger had gone and I had forgotten to notice how I coped with it, I realised that for years, I had been turning the anger on myself and harming myself with more intense smoking. I then absolutely knew that smoking was not the answer to anger.

As I have been describing my little struggles on my path to freedom you will notice that there was a lot of thinking going on. A friend of mine had stopped smoking years ago and I asked him how he had done it. He told me that he just didn't think about it. Whenever thoughts about smoking came up, he just refused to think about it and did something else to occupy his mind instead. I didn't ask, so I can only presume that six months later when he started smoking again he hadn't thought about it. It is futile trying not to think about it. Let me ask you to not think about rice pudding. You see, it's impossible. Now we've brought it up of course you're going to think about it, there is simply no choice in the matter.

Now please say out loud six times – just do it!

> **These** feelings and this confusion will pass whether I smoke or not.
> These feelings and this confusion **will** pass whether I smoke or not.
> These feelings and this confusion will **pass** whether I smoke or not.
> These feelings and this confusion will pass **whether** I smoke or not.
> These feelings and this confusion will pass whether **I** smoke or not.
> These feelings and this confusion will pass whether I smoke **or not**.

You have worked through this course, you have done the work, you don't need luck. So, my very best wishes to you.

The end.

www.StopSmokingPlan.org